INTERNET SURF AND TURF—REVEALED
The Essential Guide to Copyright, Fair Use, and Finding Media

INTERNET SURF AND TURF—REVEALED

The Essential Guide to Copyright, Fair Use, and Finding Media

By Barbara M. Waxer and Marsha L. Baum

THOMSON
™
COURSE TECHNOLOGY

Internet Surf and Turf—Revealed: The Essential Guide to Copyright, Fair Use, and Finding Media

Barbara M. Waxer, Marsha L. Baum

Managing Editor:
Marjorie Hunt

Senior Product Manager:
Christina Kling Garrett

Associate Product Manager:
Shana Rosenthal

Editorial Assistant:
Janine Tangney

Marketing Manager:
Joy Stark

Marketing Coordinator:
Melissa Marcoux

Production Editor:
Philippa Lehar

Developmental Editor:
MT Cozzola

Composition House:
GEX Publishing Services

QA Manuscript Reviewers:
John Freitas, Danielle Shaw,
Jeff Schwartz

Conceptual Artist:
Anita Quintana—Media Mantis

Text Designer:
Ann Small

Illustrator:
Michael Morgenstern

Cover Design:
Steve Deschene

Copy Editor:
Mark Goodin

Proofreader:
Harold Johnson

Indexer:
Rich Carlson

ILLUSTRATION CREDITS

About This Book

The Revealed Series is your guide to today's hottest multimedia applications and topics. The issue of copyright infringement is a very hot topic that is not only important to multimedia students, but also to students in all disciplines across the country. With copyright owners filing lawsuits because of their concern about the ease with which students can download or share copyrighted works without permission, it's clear that students need to arm themselves with a basic understanding and respect for copyright so that they don't find themselves (or their school) involved in a lawsuit.

Internet Surf and Turf—Revealed: The Essential Guide to Copyright, Fair Use, and Finding Media bridges the gap between the multimedia and design communities and the legal framework under which they work. The content is presented in a highly visual and accessible way to give students practical insights and tools they can use.

—The Revealed Series

Authors' Vision and Dedication

Like many students and professionals who use the Internet to find art and media, I've been stymied by the difficulty of finding sites with public domain files, ignorant about copyright law, and confused over how or whether I could use a file under fair use, whatever that was. My experience is hardly unique; this summarizes the experience of the majority of students and workers who ever use the Internet to find artwork or media. With *Surf and Turf*, we address these concerns and more by combining three key elements. First, we present an overview of intellectual property law tailored for Internet images and media. It is designed to give the reader basic tools for understanding copyright infringement, determining how and whether to use a file, and ensuring copyright protection for their own work. Second, we've combined that knowledge with a short but relevant Internet history and lessons guiding the reader to downloadable files from many different sites. Last of all, we've compiled the most comprehensive online resource of sites offering public domain or open access files.

The genesis of this book occurred a couple years ago while I was writing *Macromedia Fireworks MX 2004—Design Professional*. My thanks to Jane Hosie-Bounar for offering sensible feedback to my tales of artwork woe, which led me to expanding and researching an idea and then pitching it to Managing Editor Nicole Pinard, and later to her successor, Marjorie Hunt. I am incredibly grateful for Marjorie's instantaneous interest in the project and openness to letting me color way outside the lines. She assumed all the risk and continually championed this book through every publishing and marketing layer. Our Product Manager, Christina Kling-Garrett, set up an incredible team and has been a steadfast navigator. I so appreciate her skills as both project advocate and devil's advocate. Kudos to Art Director Deborah van Rooyen for directing a fabulous cover design and to Michael Morgenstern for developing the inspirational artwork found on each chapter opener and the book cover and to Joy Stark, for her enthusiasm and marketing creativity. Thanks to our reviewers, Dedree Drees, Susan Oakes, and Ken Wade for their in-depth commentary, to Rachel Bunin, our unflappable permissions wrangler, and to Anita Quintana of Media Mantis for crystal-clear conceptual art. Our amazing Production Editor Philippa Lehar kept pulling rabbits out of hats, Jill Klaffky and Aimee Poirier filled in seamlessly, and Mark Goodin was both copy editor and ocean surfing authority. MT Cozzola, our Development Editor, enriched this book in countless ways; she is extraordinarily talented. I am indebted to Marsha Baum for taking a huge leap of faith in joining this project. Marsha was exceptionally patient trying to teach me intellectual

property law, and then fixing my often mangled interpretation of her concise, well-organized background notes. My deepest appreciation always to my partner, Lindy, for maintaining our warm and nurturing home, even when I decorate it in piles of paper.
—Barbara Waxer

Thanks to Barbara Waxer for the vision for this book and for allowing me to be a part of it. Thank you to Brian Grayson for his excellent research assistance. To Sol Davis, Barry Berenberg, and Koury Hicks: thanks for your examples. Thank you to the terrific team at Course Technology for their guidance through the publication process. A special thank you to my husband, Richard Klingler, who took over much of the care for our one-year old daughters, Amanda and Elise Klingler, while I worked on the book. You three are the loves of my life.
—Marsha L. Baum

Many thanks go to Patty Gillilan, Sinclair Community College; Diane Hudson, Middlesex Community College; Constance Humphries, AB Tech; and Mike Michaelson, Palomar College for their comments in the initial stages of development. Their thoughts and ideas were extremely helpful in shaping in the book.

Our chapter reviewers, Dedree Drees, Community Colleges of Baltimore County; Susan Oakes, Briarcliff College; and Ken Wade, Champlain College deserve many kudos for their comments and keeping up with our schedule despite moving, and torrential downpours in other countries!

Thanks to Brian Grayson, Legal Research Assistant, for his help in researching the information for the timelines and the International appendix.

SERIES & AUTHORS' VISION

What Instructor Resources Are Available with This Book?

The Instructor Resources CD-ROM is Thomson Course Technology's way of putting the resources and information needed to teach and learn effectively into your hands. All the resources are available for both Macintosh and Windows operating systems, and many of the resources can be downloaded from *www.course.com*.

Instructor's Manual

Available as an electronic file, the Instructor's Manual is quality-assurance tested and includes chapter overviews and detailed lecture topics for each chapter, with teaching tips. The Instructor's Manual is available on the Instructor Resources CD-ROM, or you can download it from *www.course.com*.

Syllabus

Prepare and customize your course easily using this sample course outline (available on the Instructor Resources CD-ROM).

PowerPoint Presentations

Each chapter has a corresponding PowerPoint presentation that you can use in lectures, distribute to your students, or customize to suit your course.

Figure Files

Figure Files contain all the figures from the book in bitmap format. Use the figure files to create transparency masters or include them in a PowerPoint presentation.

Solutions to Projects

Sample solutions to all end of chapter material are provided. Use these files to evaluate your students' work. Or, distribute them electronically or in hard copy so students can verify their work.

Test Bank and Test Engine

ExamView is a powerful testing software package that allows instructors to create and administer printed, computer (LAN-based), and Internet exams. ExamView includes hundreds of questions that correspond to the topics covered in this text, enabling students to generate detailed study guides that include page references for further review. The computer-based and Internet testing components allow students to take exams at their computers, and also saves the instructor time by grading each exam automatically.

Online Content

This book has considerable online content which you can access by navigating to *www.course.com/revealed/surfandturf*. This site has several sections of interest:

- The *Online Companion* lists links to sites referenced in the lessons and projects.

- The *Surf and Turf Index of Online Resources* (STIOR) provides links to dozens of public domain and open access sites. It is publicly available. We encourage users to expand this online resource by submitting sites to include or delete.

- An appendix on International Copyright Law, discussing the significant provisions of international treaties and of individual countries.

CHAPTER 1   UNDERSTANDING COPYRIGHT

LESSON 1
Understand Intellectual Property Law 5
Understanding Intellectual Property 5
Origins of Intellectual Property Law 6
The Categories of Intellectual Property 7
Who Regulates Intellectual
Property Law? 10

LESSON 2
Understand the Purpose of Copyright 11
Evolution of Copyright Law 11
Ramifications of Law and Court Cases 16
Ramifications of Digital Technology 18
Copyright Term Extensions 19
Musicians and Royalties 20
Balancing Protection and Innovation 21

LESSON 3
Understand Copyright Protection 22
How Copyright Affects Society 22
What Does Copyright Protect? 22
When Does Copyright Protection Begin? 23
What Makes Copyright Protection
Obtainable? 23
What Is Not Protected? 25

LESSON 4
Understand Copyright Ownership 26
Understanding Copyright Transfer 26
Understanding Work for Hire 26
What Exactly Does the Copyright
Owner Own? 27

LESSON 5
Understand International Copyright 29
Understanding International Copyright 29

LESSON 6
Understand How to Protect Work 32
Understanding Copyright Registration 32
Registering Copyright 33
Posting a Copyright Notice 34
Understanding Watermarks 34

CHAPTER 2   UNDERSTANDING INFRINGEMENT AND FAIR USE

LESSON 1
Understand Infringement 43
What Is Infringement? 43
Copyright Infringement 43
The Many Shades of Infringement 44
Derivative Works: A Difficult Balance
of Rights 46
Internet Innovations and Copyright Law 47
Right of Publicity and Privacy
Infringement 49
Right of Publicity Violations 50
Nonviolations of Rights of Publicity 51

LESSON 2
Understand Fair Use 53
The Fair Use Doctrine 53
Personal Responsibilities 56
Educational Responsibilities 56
Trademark Fair Use 58
The Strongest Trademark that
Almost Wasn't 58
Exploring Important Court Cases 59

LESSON 3
Understand Infringement Legalities 64
Understanding the Legal Setting for
Infringement Suits 64
What Must Be Proven to Make a Case? 64
Chilling Effects: Where Politics Meets
Reality 65
What Will Happen if You Infringe
Copyright 66

LESSON 4
Understand the Public Domain 68
Public Domain Works 68
The Merger Doctrine 68
Abandonment of Copyright by Donation 70
Moving In and Out of Public Domain 70

CHAPTER 3 SEARCHING THE INTERNET

LESSON 1
Understand the Internet Timeline 78
Inspiration for the Internet 78
Early Internet Development 80
Emergence of the World Wide Web 80
Evolution of Web Addresses 82
Breakthroughs for Public Web Users 82
The Difference Between the Internet and
the Web 83
Internet Milestone Trivia 84

LESSON 2
**Understand Internet Search Engines
and Tools** 85
The History of Searching the Internet 85
What Is a Search Engine? 86
How an Index Search Engine Works 86
How Directories Work 87
How Pay-Per-Click Searches Work 87
The Open Directory Project 88
How Search Engines Differ 89
Understanding Meta Tags 91
Untangling the Relationship Between
Search Engines 92
Understanding Meta Search Engines 93
Can You Ever Really Search the Web? 94

LESSON 3
Perform Simple Searches 95
Using Keywords 95
Tasks Perform a keyword search 97
       Add a keyword to search criteria 98

LESSON 4
Perform Advanced Searches 99
Using Advanced Search Features 99
Boolean Operators 100
Tasks Use an image search tool 102
       Use advanced search features 103
       Construct a complex search 104

LESSON 5
Search the Invisible Web 105
About the Invisible Web 105
Tasks Search the invisible Web 107
       Search for databases 108

**CHAPTER 4 FINDING AND ACQUIRING IMAGES
AND MEDIA**

INTRODUCTION
Finding Sites 116

LESSON 1
**Understand Licenses and
Permissions** 119
Determining Use 119
Understanding Licensing Agreements 119
Understanding Terms of Use 121
Locating Terms of Use 122
Obtaining Permission or a License 122
Locating Whom to Ask 123
Acquiring Different Copyright Licenses 125
Task Review terms of use 128

LESSON 2
Understand Media Files 129
Understanding File Types 129
Understanding Optimization and
Resolution 133

LESSON 3
Find Clip Art and Web Art 134
Finding Clip Art and Web Art on the Web 134
Tasks Find clip art 135
       Find animation 136

LESSON 4
Find Photographs 138
Finding Photographs on the Web 138
Understanding Blogs 139

Understanding RSS Feeds 140
Understanding Podcasting 141
Using Government Resources 141
Restricting Image Content 142
Tasks Find public domain photos 143
       Find photos with mixed licensing 144
       Search a government site for public
       domain photos 146

LESSON 5
Find Video 147
Finding Movie Files 147
Task Find video 148

LESSON 6
Find Audio 149
Finding Audio Files 149
Tasks Find sound effects 150
       Find music 151

LESSON 7
Find Media at the Library of Congress 153
Understanding the Library of Congress 153
Navigating the Library of Congress 153
National Archives 154
Tasks Find photos at the Library of Congress 155
       Search for video at the Library of
       Congress 157
Glossary 164
Index 168

Baseline Assumptions

This book is a resource for computer users of all skill levels, but we do assume basic word processing and computer skills sufficient for navigating to a URL and copying and pasting. As you navigate to the various Web sites, remember that Web pages and content update constantly, so what you see on the screen will probably not match what you see on the page. Also be aware that educational institution, government, or company computer and Internet policies may limit access to the Internet and affect your ability to complete all the lessons. We also assume that appropriate search filters are active when using search engines. We strongly encourage you to open the Preferences or Advanced pages of search engines if you are not familiar with these settings.

Using the Online Companion

When directed to the Online Companion in the text, follow these steps: Connect to the Internet, go to www.course.com/revealed/surfandturf (the page containing all online content for this book), click the Online Companion link, and then click the appropriate link.

Legal Disclaimer

This book concentrates on copyright and trademark law as the two types of intellectual property law that will have the most impact on Web designers, artists, and anyone using Internet images and media. This book does not provide legal advice and use of this book does not establish an attorney-client relationship. It provides an overview of the law and offers examples, but does not provide comprehensive coverage on the nuances of copyright or trademark law. For specific legal questions and concerns, consult your lawyer.

READ THIS BEFORE YOU BEGIN

chapter 1

UNDERSTANDING
Copyright

1. Understand intellectual property law.

2. Understand the purpose of copyright.

3. Understand copyright protection.

4. Understand copyright ownership.

5. Understand international copyright.

6. Understand how to protect work.

chapter 1 UNDERSTANDING Copyright

Gaining a cursory but working understanding of the history of copyright law provides a context for your interaction with current and future changes in this field.

Drawing heavily on its British roots since its founding, the United States has institutionalized intellectual property; it was written into the Constitution. However, it is by no means a static entity. The driving forces of any time and age create the conditions for legal change, and intellectual property law continues to evolve as the forces of technology, culture, and commerce shift and develop. There is no doubt that copyright law will continue to change significantly, perhaps even by the time this book is printed.

Each type of law in this country has its associated legal history and social issues. Among these, intellectual property law holds a unique niche. Not only do segments of society question the purpose of intellectual property, they question its very right to exist. For many, the presence or absence of intellectual property *is* the argument.

How you feel about copyright infringement depends on the role you might play in the infringement scenario. Being knowledgeable about what constitutes copyright infringement can inform and empower your decision making.

UNDERSTAND
Intellectual Property Law

What You'll Learn

▶ *In this lesson, you will learn about intellectual property and the categories that make up intellectual property law in the United States.*

Understanding Intellectual Property

The term *intellectual property* immediately imparts gravitas, even if you have absolutely no idea what it means; but the word *intellectual* simply serves to distinguish this type of property from physical property. **Intellectual property** is a product resulting from human creativity. It can include inventions, movies, songs, designs, clothing, and so on—anything created through intellectual or mental labor, as opposed to being constructed out of physical components. Unlike real property (better known as real estate), or personal property (better known as your stuff), intellectual property refers to intangible assets. For example, if you design a new chair, your design is an **intangible asset**—it conveys the idea of the chair and specifications for how the chair should be built. If you manufacture the chair and sell it to your neighbors, the chair becomes part of their personal property.

Intellectual property law establishes how and when a person and society as a whole can benefit and profit from someone's creation. Treating intangible ideas the same as tangible property can be problematic. The claims of ownership between tangible and intangible property are similar, but it is impossible to apply all the rules of intellectual property to real property, and vice versa. For example, if you own a home on the beach in southern California, you can keep it as long you want and make plans to leave it to your heirs. However, if the house and beach disappear after an earthquake, your heirs inherit nothing, because there is nothing tangible left for them to inherit (insurance claims not withstanding). Not so with some intellectual property; intangible property cannot disappear. Under present law, some intellectual property rights are protected for decades after your death—your heirs can continue to benefit from your ideas for years. This is one aspect of intellectual property that makes its laws so contentious as they play out against a constantly changing world.

Origins of Intellectual Property Law

The foundation upon which copyright and patent law in the United States is based was written directly into the Constitution, as shown in Figure 1; Article 1, Section 8, Clause 8 is nestled in between Congress's power to establish post offices and establish federal district courts:

Congress has the power to promote the Progress of Science and useful Arts, by securing for limited Times to Authors and Inventors the exclusive Right to their respective Writings and Discoveries.

The purpose of its inclusion was two-fold: to protect the creations of individuals by giving them a monopoly on their work for a set amount of time; and then to dissolve that monopoly by allowing the work to be accessed by the public, which presumably would build upon and improve the work.

It is the latter purpose upon which our tradition of intellectual property has developed. In fact, Clause 8 became known as the "Progress Clause," as opposed to the "Protection Clause." Today, many are concerned that the law has shifted emphasis to protecting intellectual property rights over promoting use. Some estimate that more changes have been made to intellectual property law in the past 20 years than were made over the previous 200.

FIGURE 1
U.S. Constitution

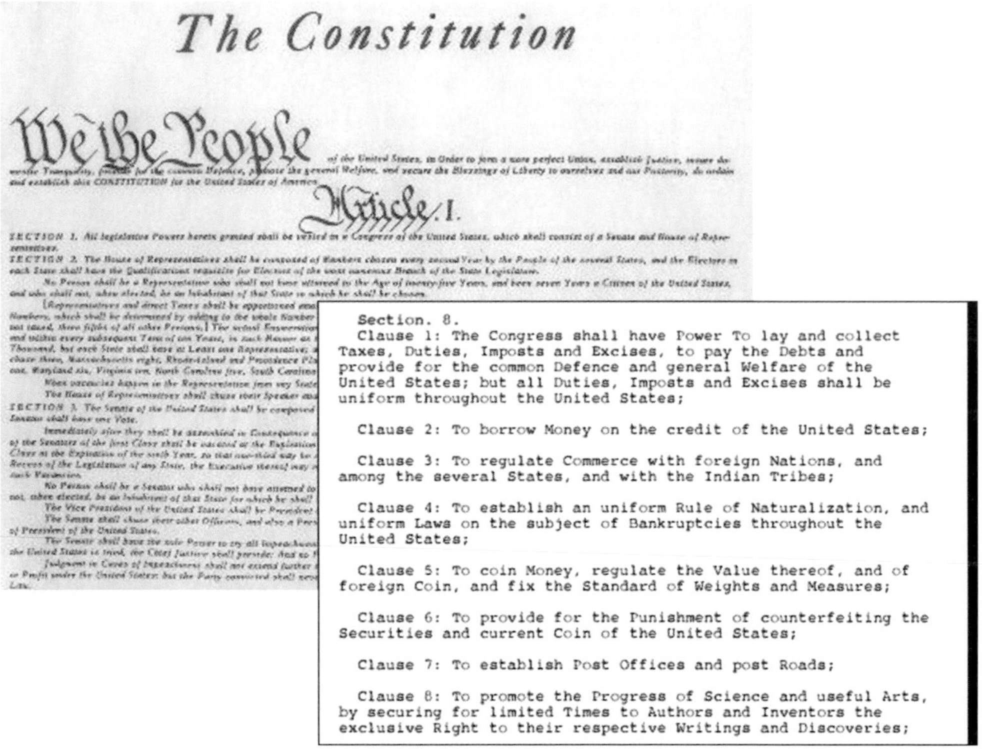

Section. 8.
Clause 1: The Congress shall have Power To lay and collect Taxes, Duties, Imposts and Excises, to pay the Debts and provide for the common Defence and general Welfare of the United States; but all Duties, Imposts and Excises shall be uniform throughout the United States;

Clause 2: To borrow Money on the credit of the United States;

Clause 3: To regulate Commerce with foreign Nations, and among the several States, and with the Indian Tribes;

Clause 4: To establish an uniform Rule of Naturalization, and uniform Laws on the subject of Bankruptcies throughout the United States;

Clause 5: To coin Money, regulate the Value thereof, and of foreign Coin, and fix the Standard of Weights and Measures;

Clause 6: To provide for the Punishment of counterfeiting the Securities and current Coin of the United States;

Clause 7: To establish Post Offices and post Roads;

Clause 8: To promote the Progress of Science and useful Arts, by securing for limited Times to Authors and Inventors the exclusive Right to their respective Writings and Discoveries;

The Categories of Intellectual Property

Intellectual property is divided into categories. Each category represents particular protection over particular products:

- **Copyright law** protects the expression of an idea but not the underlying idea itself, in a rule of law known as the Idea-Expression Dichotomy. That is, the subject matter is not afforded copyright protection, but the manner in which you express it is. For example, imagine you write a story about discovering the lost city of Atlantis. The idea of discovering Atlantis is not afforded copyright protection, but no one else could use your specific plot and characters. Copyright law provides protection for a minimum term of the life of the author plus 70 years (or 95 years in the case of anonymous or pseudonymous works) against others using the work unless an exception such as fair use applies. **Fair use** allows limited use of copyrighted materials without permission of the copyright holder.

- **Patent law** provides monopoly protection for inventions that meet the requirements of utility, novelty, and nonobviousness, meaning your invention is useful, out of the ordinary, and would be an unexpected or surprising development to people working in the field. Patents have been used for everything from nanotechnology that integrates materials onto a silicon wafer to antiwrinkle creams to a ventilated storage container designed to protect a banana in transit (see Figure 2). While patent protection doesn't last as long as copyright protection, patent protection

FIGURE 2
Sample products and services

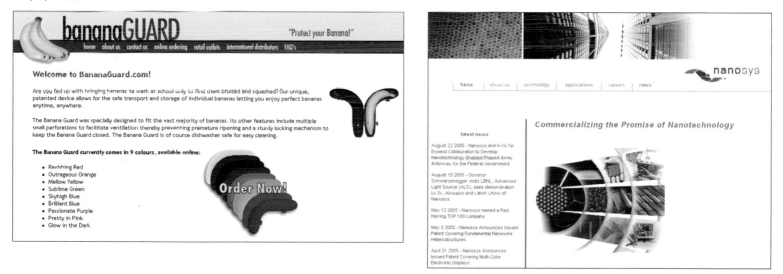

is much stronger than copyright protection. The patent holder has exclusive rights to produce, use, or sell the invention.

■ **Trademark law** allows entities engaged in commerce to exclusively protect a particular word, symbol, or design to identify their goods or services. Protection related to services is known as a service mark. The mark is protected under state common law and eligible for federal registration, as long as it is distinctive and is not confusingly similar to marks currently in use. The Nike swoosh or the MGM roaring lion are immediately recognizable, as are other trademark examples shown in Figure 3. Table 1 describes the symbols associated with trademark and copyright.

■ **Trade secret law** is protection under state law against unauthorized use of secret business information such as a secret formula for a protein drink. However, the secret stays with you—you do not have to transmit it for registration.

■ **Trade dress law** protects the appearance and image of a product or service, such as its packaging size and shape or the color combinations. Examples include

FIGURE 3
Sample trademarks

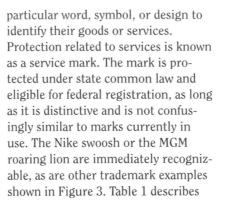

The politics of patent filing
The United States is the only country whose patent doctrine is based on first to invent rather than first to file. In 1876, Alexander Graham Bell beat out Elisha Gray for a patent on the telephone by two hours even though it would be years before Bell produced one that worked. Adding to the intrigue was Gray's patent application design of a unique variable resistance transmitter, which was later found to be written in the margin of Bell's patent application.

décor, such as the Outback Steakhouse chain, or the unique shape of a classic Coca Cola bottle.

- A **design patent** protects the "new, original and ornamental design for an article of manufacture" that meets the patent requirements of novelty and nonobviousness. Examples include the design for the latest basketball shoe or coffee maker.

- **Right of publicity** and **right of privacy** protect an individual person under state law. The right of publicity protects against the use of an individual's likeness for commercial advantage. This right is asserted by celebrities who are in a position to lose financially from the unauthorized use of their identities.

The right of privacy protects individuals from interference with their right to be left alone and to protect themselves from publicity that presents embarrassing personal facts or that misrepresents the person. Tabloid newspapers and television shows often press the limits of both laws.

TABLE 1: Trademark and Copyright Symbols

symbol	type	use when
®	Trademark	Registered with U.S. Patent Office
TM	Trademark	Not registered with U.S. Patent Office
SM	Service mark	Not registered with U.S. Patent Office
©	Copyright	Necessary for copyrighted works created prior to 3/1/89; since 1989, optional for all works
℗	Copyright	Sound recording copyright

Comparing copyright, patents, and trade secrets

Copyright provides a longer period of protection—the life of the author plus 70 years—compared to 20 years for a patent (or 14 years for a design patent, which covers the aesthetics and appearance of an object, not its function). Patents provide stronger protection than trade secrets and copyright, but are made public through the application process at the Patent Office. However, patent law prohibits someone from reverse engineering the invention for which a patent has been issued. Trade secrets do not require any registration, can be kept secret forever, and anyone—an employee, former employee, or hacker—who discloses or sells the trade secret information can be prosecuted.

Who Regulates Intellectual Property Law?

Some areas of intellectual property law are governed by federal agencies while others are regulated by state government. The protections offered by the law differ for each category; some are federal protections and some are state protections, as shown in Figure 4. Of course, because states enact their own laws and statutes, those protections can vary and even contradict each other.

FIGURE 4
Regulating intellectual property law

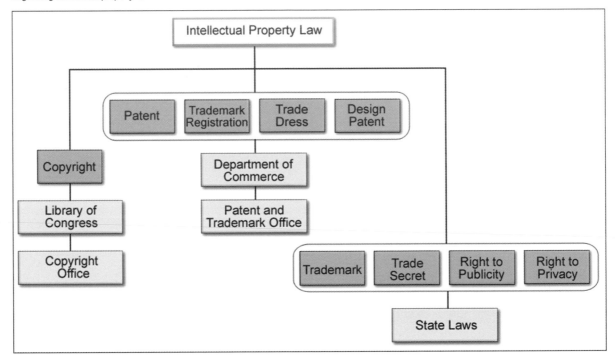

What You'll Learn

In this lesson, you will learn about the principles associated with copyright.

FIGURE 5
Timeline linking technology to copyright law

UNDERSTAND THE PURPOSE
of Copyright

Evolution of Copyright Law

The origins of copyright law can be traced to long before this country was founded, as the timeline in Figure 5 depicts. American copyright law is traced directly to the British legal tradition. British copyright law was developed in the sixteenth century after the introduction of what was then bleeding-edge technology, the printing press. For hundreds of years, British printers held absolute monopolies over all printing and the distribution of books, a right bestowed on them by the monarchy. Copyright was originally used to censor what was written by controlling who could print books. That came to halt in 1710 when the Statute of Anne, shown in Figure 6, provided authors with something unheard at the time: exclusive rights over their own works for 14 years and an optional renewal of another 14 if the author was still alive. Following the

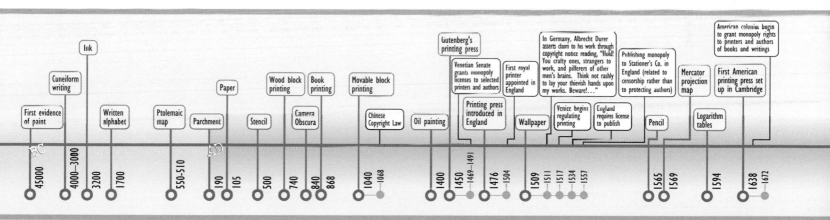

term of copyright protection, a work would pass into the **public domain**, meaning that it is available to anyone for copying, altering, distributing (for profit or not), and so on, without restriction. After the American Revolution, the fledgling government maintained much of the British standard.

Because initial copyright applied only to written works but today protects work by artists, designers, songwriters, and so on, the term **author** is used to refer to anyone creating a work of intellectual property. Table 2 shows the highlights of changes made to U.S. copyright law over the past 200 years. Many of the amendments to the Act reflected new technology and art forms, as the timeline below illustrates.

QUICK**TIP**

The first U.S. copyright entry was for *The Philadelphia Spelling Book* by John Barry, registered on June 9, 1790.

FIGURE 6
Statute of Anne

Anno Octavo
Annæ Reginæ.

An Act for the Encouragement of Learning, by Vesting the Copies of Printed Books in the Authors or Purchasers of such Copies, during the Times therein mentioned.

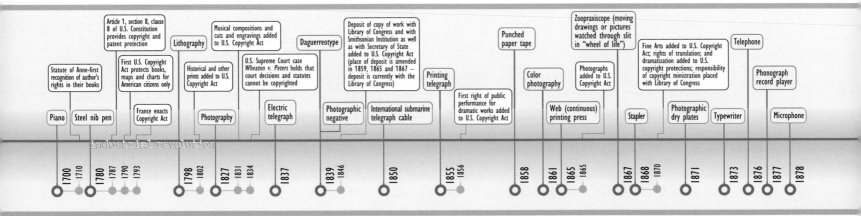

TABLE 2: Significant Changes in U.S. Copyright Law

act	works included	copyright term	effect
Act of 1790	Books, maps, charts	14 yrs + 14 yr renewal	If author still alive and a U.S. resident or citizen
1802	Prints		
1831	Musical compositions	28 yrs + 14 yr renewal	Widows and children included
1856	Public performances of dramatic works		
1865	Photographs		
1870	Fine art: paintings, sculpture, designs, drawings		
Copyright Act of 1909		28 yrs + 28 yr renewal	Protection began upon publication, not registration; state laws protected unpublished works
Copyright Act of 1976	Original works of authorship	Life of author + 50 yrs	Copyright upon fixation in a tangible medium of expression; limits on author's exclusive rights established through fair use, nonprofit, educational, library, and religious exemptions; authors could license parts of work and retain rights
Visual Artists Rights Act of 1990			Granted right to fine artists to remove their names from works that had been changed or used without authorization

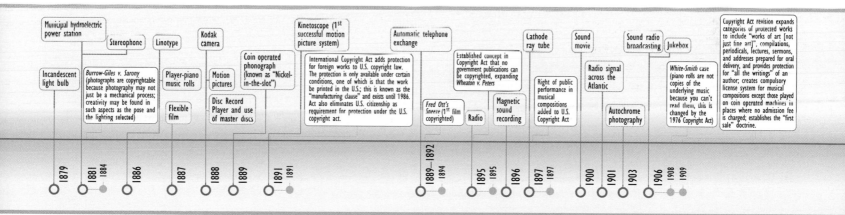

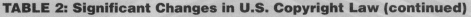

TABLE 2: Significant Changes in U.S. Copyright Law (continued)

act	works included	copyright term	effect
Architectual Works Copyright Protection Act of 1990	Design of a building		
Computer Software Rental Amendment of 1990 & Record Rental Amendment of 1984	Copyright owner given exclusive control over rental of computer programs and sound recordings		
Audio Home Recording Act of 1992	Digital audio transmission		Manufacturers installed anticopying technology in exchange for the recording industry not suing the public for home recording
Uruguay Round Agreements Act of 1994			Restored copyright to non-U.S. works not previously protected
Sonny Bono Copyright Term Extension Act of 1998		Life of author + 70 yrs; 95 years for work for hire, anonymous, or pseudonymous works	Extended copyright protection by 20 years to new and existing works that were in copyright (retroactive extension)

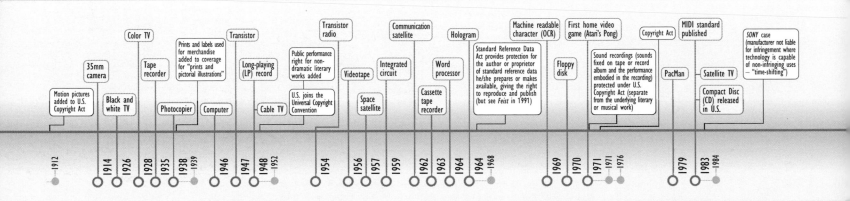

TABLE 2: Significant Changes in U.S. Copyright Law (continued)

act	works included	copyright term	effect
Digital Millennium Copyright Act of 1998			Prohibited the acts of bypassing encryption or anticopying systems and of removing copyright management information and provided protections for Internet service providers
TEACH Act of 2002			Extended educational exemption to distance learning environments
Family Entertainment and Copyright Act of 2005	Unreleased film and music		Made it a crime to tape movies in a theater or share on a network an unreleased film or song, and allowed use of hardware that can skip and mute DVDs

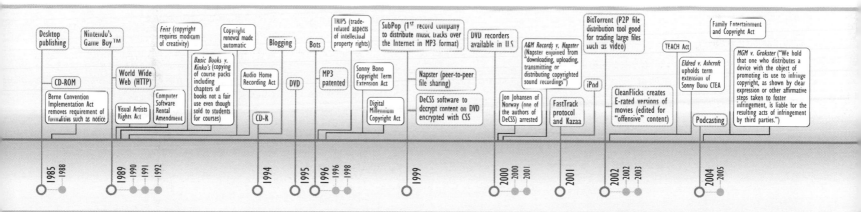

Desktop publishing

Nintendo's Game Boy ™

Feist (copyright requires modicum of creativity)

Copyright renewal made automatic

Blogging

Bots

TRIPS (trade-related aspects of intellectual property rights)

SubPop (1st record company to distribute music tracks over the Internet in MP3 format)

DVD recorders available in U.S.

BitTorrent (P2P file distribution tool good for trading large files such as video)

Family Entertainment and Copyright Act

CD-ROM

Berne Convention Implementation Act removes requirement of formalities such as notice

World Wide Web (HTTP)

Visual Artists Rights Act

Computer Software Rental Amendment

Basic Books v. Kinko's (copying of course packs including chapters of books not a fair use even though sold to students for courses)

Audio Home Recording Act

CD-R

DVD

MP3 patented

Sonny Bono Copyright Term Extension Act

Digital Millennium Copyright Act

Napster (peer-to-peer file sharing)

DeCSS software to decrypt content on DVD encrypted with CSS

A&M Records v. Napster (Napster enjoined from "downloading, uploading, transmitting or distributing copyrighted sound recordings")

Jon Johansen of Norway (one of the authors of DeCSS) arrested

FastTrack protocol and Kazaa

iPod

CleanFlicks creates E-rated versions of movies (edited for "offensive" content)

TEACH Act

Eldred v. Ashcroft upholds term extension of Sonny Bono CTEA

Podcasting

MGM v. Grokster ("We hold that one who distributes a device with the object of promoting its use to infringe copyright, as shown by clear expression or other affirmative steps taken to foster infringement, is liable for the resulting acts of infringement by third parties.")

1985 1988 1989 1990 1991 1992 1994 1995 1996 1996 1998 1999 2000 2000 2001 2001 2002 2002 2003 2004 2005

Ramifications of Law and Court Cases

As we review the changes to copyright law, one recurring theme emerges: the rights of authors have increased dramatically over time, resulting in conflicts over a copyright owner's economic rights and the intent of the Progress Clause to nurture the public good.

The Copyright Act of 1976 codified established case law (the body of law created by court decisions) by adding a statutory provision for fair use, which is discussed at length in Chapter 2. It also eliminated the requirement to register a copyright for a work in order for the work to have copyright protection.

External factors also appear to influence new laws, such as the 20-year copyright extension offered in the Sonny Bono Copyright Term Extension Act (CTEA) of 1998. The copyright law had just undergone a massive overhaul 22 years earlier. When CTEA was introduced in Congress, large and powerful entertainment and media companies led lobbying efforts to extend copyright terms. Some critics of CTEA point to entertainment companies such as The Walt Disney Company, which has made billions by borrowing creatively and substantially from existing public domain works, including the following examples:

- Fairy and folk tales (long in the public domain), such as Snow White and the Seven Dwarfs, Cinderella, Beauty and the Beast, Bambi, and Mulan.
- Books, such as *The Adventures of Pinocchio*, which, had it been under the copyright terms of the Bono Act, would not have entered the public domain until 1960. (Disney made its animated *Pinocchio* in 1940.)
- Musical compositions such as Fantasia's use of Modest Mussorgsky's Night on Bald Mountain, which itself had been previously rearranged by Nikolai Rimsky-Korsakov.

At the time CTEA was introduced, the rights to Mickey Mouse were set to expire in 2003, with other characters such as Pluto, Goofy, and Donald Duck due to pass a few years later. Suffice it to say, Disney had enormous financial incentive to retain exclusive rights for these characters. Under the new terms of the CTEA, no copyrighted work, from Disney or anyone else, will enter the public domain until 2019, which affects tens of thousands of works and millions of users who could otherwise use and build upon those works. By contrast, during this same time period, it is estimated that over one million patents will pass in to the public domain.

QUICK**TIP**

Any copyright holder can choose to donate their work to the public domain or make it available through an open access license; you learn more about this topic in Chapter 4.

CTEA also set in motion a case that made it to the Supreme Court, whose ruling greatly affected copyright law. *Eldred v. Ashcroft* questioned whether Congress's right to extend copyright terms was constitutional. Eric Eldred published public domain books online with hyperlinks and the ability to cross-reference through Eldtritch Press. His point: if Congress is allowed to keep extending copyright terms, then nothing will ever pass into the public domain, which violates the Progress Clause and First Amendment of the Constitution. CTEA's terms not only pertained to new works, they renewed the copyright of existing works, which retroactively extended their copyright. Therefore, works that were about to enter the public domain, and the people whose livelihoods depended on public domain works (such as Eldred) were going to lose out until 2019. The Court ruled in a 7–2 decision that Congress was within its mandate to extend copyright extension as long as the extension was for a limited time. The two dissenting opinions argued that unlimited term extensions were not in the tradition of the Progress Clause and that the current terms were so long as be effectively unlimited, which was unconstitutional. The dates works enter the public domain are shown in Figure 7. The terms of copyright are shown in Figure 8.

FIGURE 7
Public domain dates

Date	Enters Public Domain
Published before 1923	In public domain
Published from 1923-63	In public domain if not renewed; otherwise as late as 2059
Published from 1964-77	Approximately 2060 or later
Created before 1-1-78 but not published	Some in public domain, others as long as approximately 2110
Created before 1-1-78 but published between then and 12-31-2002	2047 to approximately 2110
Created 1-1-78 or after	2011 or later

years are based on personal not corporate authors and assume the earliest copyright protection is granted at 18 and an author's life span is 80 years

FIGURE 8
When U.S. works pass into public domain

by Lolly Gasaway   University of North Carolina

Date of Work	Protected From	Term
Created 1-1-78 or after	When work is fixed in tangible medium of expression	Life + 70 years[1] (or if work of corporate authorship, the shorter of 95 years from publication, or 120 years from creation[2])
Published before 1923	In public domain	None
Published from 1923-63	When published with notice[3]	28 years + could be renewed for 47 years, now extended by 20 years for a total renewal of 67 years. If not so renewed, now in public domain
Published from 1964-77	When published with notice	28 years for first term; now automatic extension of 67 years for second term
Created before 1-1-78 but not published	1-1-78, the effective date of the 1976 Act which eliminated common law copyright	Life + 70 years or 12-31-2002, whichever is greater
Created before 1-1-78 but published between then and 12-31-2002	1-1-78, the effective date of the 1976 Act which eliminated common law copyright	Life + 70 years or 12-31-2047, whichever is greater

1 Term of joint works is measured by life of the longest-lived author.
2 Works for hire, anonymous and pseudonymous works also have this term. 17 U.S.C. § 302(c).
3 Under the 1909 Act, works published without notice went into the public domain upon publication. Works published without notice between 1-1-78 and 3-1-89, effective date of the Berne Convention Implementation Act, retained copyright only if efforts to correct the accidental omission of notice was made within five years, such as by placing notice on unsold copies. 17 U.S.C. § 405. (Notes courtesy of Professor Tom Field, Franklin Pierce Law Center and Lolly Gasaway)

Ramifications of Digital Technology

The precedent for digital technologies was set in 1984 with *SONY v. Universal*, when the U.S. Supreme Court ruled that consumers did not violate copyright when they recorded television programs in a practice dubbed time-shifting: record, play-back, and erase. The ruling also held that manufacturers of the hardware of the time, VCRs and Betamax, are not liable for infringement when the hardware is also capable of non-infringing uses. The ruling was strongly opposed by media corporations (even though videotape rentals and sales would go on to add significant profit to movie companies' coffers).

The precedent of the *SONY* case is no longer strictly followed. The Digital Millennium Copyright Act (DMCA) penalizes anyone who attempts to circumvent (hack) anticopying technologies on digital media. Under this law you can excerpt sections from a written book under a fair use exception, but if you create software that circumvents anti-copying measures on an e-book to allow copying of the same excerpts, you have violated the DMCA.

Similarly, the Family Entertainment and Copyright Act of 2005 (FECA) makes it a crime to record a movie in a movie theater or to share on a network a song or movie not yet released, and it allows companies to manufacture hardware that automatically skips and mutes portions of DVDs.

QUICK**TIP**

The fines or imprisonment penalties for digital theft under the FECA are exponentially higher than for shoplifting of the same material from a department store.

The main argument for prohibiting file sharing is that the technology has mainly been used to infringe on others' copyright, unlike legal precedent that had exempted VCR and DVD makers from the same claim. Under FECA, parents, specifically, can use technology that deletes content from movies they do not want their children to see, which, it is argued, exempts makers of that technology from liability for infringing on the moviemaker's copyright.

QUICK**TIP**

The process of purging content deemed undesirable is known as *bowdlerization*, named after Thomas Bowdler, who published a sanitized and censored version of Shakespearian plays in the early 1800s.

The Federal Communications Commission (FCC) passed a rule in 2003, later overturned in appellate court in 2005, that allowed television networks to embed a digital code, known as a broadcast flag, into a broadcast television show. The broadcast flag could indicate whether the program could be recorded, possibly limit the quality and media onto which the program could be recorded, and eliminate the ability of consumers to skip over commercials.

Copyright Term Extensions

Not surprisingly, in a country that supports the First Amendment there is no shortage of opinion on how long copyright protection should be granted. Proponents for extended copyright terms believe that the economic incentive copyright protection provides is not only crucial to innovation, but a right that should last into perpetuity. Congresswoman Mary Bono, widow of Sonny Bono, is quoted in the Congressional Record: "Actually, Sonny wanted the term of copyright protection to last forever. I am informed by staff that such a change would violate the Constitution...there is also Jack Valenti's proposal for *term to last forever less one day*" [emphasis added]. (For 38 years, Jack Valenti was president of the Motion Picture Association of America, an organization that represents the movie industry.)

Social issues and FECA

While the legal questions may be moot—legal software that permits severe movie editing already exists—policy questions loom large. What are the ramifications of parents or commercial sponsors being able to sanitize any content they find objectionable: censorship or the empowerment of individual values? If you don't think a film is suitable for a child, why not watch something else, discuss the content ahead of time, or wait until the child is older? What about the artistic integrity of the film: is the loss of narrative, metaphor, and message significant to one's viewing experience? Consider the impact if the last lines in *Planet of the Apes* ("You finally really did it. You maniacs! You blew it up!...") or *Gone With the Wind* ("Frankly, my dear...") or if key characters or events in *Philadelphia* or *Hotel Rwanda* were missing.

Musicians and Royalties

Many artists have been illegally denied copyright protection for their work, and many have suffered financially as a result. In the 1950s and 1960s, record companies, music publishers, and early rock and roll musicians including Elvis Presley, The Beatles, The Rolling Stones, and Cream made hits recording songs written by African-American musicians, whose royalties were simply stolen from them. Years later, successful copyright infringement suits allowed musicians such as singer Ruth Brown to recoup royalties from Atlantic Records and songwriter and bassist Willie Dixon to settle out of court with Led Zeppelin. Led Zeppelin had taken Dixon's song "You Need Love" and changed it to "Whole Lotta Love" (which has sold millions of copies since 1969). Some nonprofit organizations such as the Blues Foundation (*www.blues.org*) promote, preserve, and highlight Blues music education and history. Some have provided financial assistance to musicians, many of whom were denied royalties and copyright protections during their careers. There is no doubt that royalty payments have been a vital source of income for countless artists and other copyright owners.

FIGURE 9
The Blues Foundation

Blues Heaven Web site

Balancing Protection and Innovation

More than any other type of intellectual property, copyright protection must balance the interests of creators and society. The adaptations in copyright law in response to technological advancements demonstrate the tension between the rights of the copyright owner and the public. On one hand, protecting copyright encourages further creativity and innovation; on the other, the rights of society to utilize the creations to promote progress of science and the useful arts is required by the Constitution and, by its very action, stimulates innovation.

Copyright owners are concerned that their right to and interest in their work is at risk and that new technologies, particularly electronic communication, make it increasingly easier to transfer information and violate copyright. The ongoing controversy about file-sharing software such as peer-to-peer (P2P) exemplifies this concern. Access to and use of a work will affect revenue streams and, it is argued, ultimately limit the availability of creative works because creators would no longer be motivated to create.

Users of copyrighted information and the public at large are concerned that society's ability to use materials under copyright exemptions such as fair use and educational provisions will be eroded, and that a millennia-old tradition of borrowing and improving will be lost. This would be due in part to the public's acceptance of technologies that prevent copying, charge-per-use arrangements, and criminal penalties for downloading copyrighted material, even though simple possession of copyrighted work does not imply financial exploitation of the copyright owner.

In the legislative process, the protection of economic interests is debated against the protection of fair use and other exemptions that allow educators, libraries, and the public to use the works protected by the law. Conflicting interests result in compromises such as the TEACH Act (Technology, Education, and Copyright Harmonization), which, in return for rights to perform and display works in distance learning situations, requires that the transmitting institution put in place measures to prevent retention of the work in a form that would be readily accessible after the class has ended.

UNDERSTAND COPYRIGHT
Protection

What You'll Learn

▶ *In this lesson, you will learn about copyright protection, what is protected, when it begins, and what is not protected.*

How Copyright Affects Society

When the Copyright Act of 1909 was enacted, the lives of most Americans did not intersect with copyright law very often. Over 70 percent of the American population lived in rural areas (and most did not have electricity), 5 percent had a telephone, the movie industry had just arrived in Los Angeles, and the Ford Motor Company had sold a total of 10,000 Model T cars since its introduction a year earlier. Today, nearly 90 percent of the American population lives in urban areas, we receive and send many types of information in real time over any number of devices, and copyright impacts us throughout our day, each and every day.

What Does Copyright Protect?

As you learned earlier in this chapter, copyright protects the expression of an idea, but not the idea itself. No matter how brilliant your inspiration for a novel, process, or method, you can not prevent someone from using that idea. You may be able to patent the process or method, but you can

not protect the idea under patent law or copyright law. The same principle applies to facts: you cannot copyright facts, such as the miles per gallon for a Hummer, the number of presidents who were left-handed, sports statistics, or the number of computer-generated special effects in the latest blockbuster.

QUICK**TIP**

Generally, the laws of nature are not patentable, but their applications are. So, you could patent a design for a new roller coaster, but not the laws of physics that make it thrilling.

In 1964, Harvey Ball, an employee at State Mutual Life Insurance of Worcester, Massachusetts, was asked by management to create a company morale-building image for their "friendship campaign." He was paid $45 for drawing the ubiquitous yellow smiley face, which became a popular button for the company. In the early 1970s, two Spanish brothers combined the image with the saccharine slogan *Have a Nice Day*, but they never obtained copyright on the image, only the slogan. Use of the smiley face mushroomed throughout the 1970s, and eventually became the prototype Web emoticon. Today, there are millions of derivative smiley faces, a few of which are shown in Figure 10. In 1971, a French entrepreneur named Franklin Loufrani registered the smiley face as a trademark in over 80 countries, from which he continues to receive royalty payments—but not from the United States.

When Does Copyright Protection Begin?

Copyright protection begins *as soon as* the work is fixed, whether it is a graphic you draw in a computer program, the origami you folded to keep awake in class, or the lyrics of a new song you scribbled on the back of a concert ticket. Copyright is, therefore, implicit for every work you see on the Web, unless the owner specifically states otherwise or the work is in the public domain.

What Makes Copyright Protection Obtainable?

Copyright protects your original work of authorship fixed in any tangible medium of expression. To understand what is protected, you need to understand the legal definitions of "original," "work of authorship," and "fixed in a tangible medium of expression."

The work must be **original**—a product of the author, although not necessarily novel

FIGURE 10
Variations on a smiley face

or unique. It can be similar to existing works (such as two people photographing the same scene) and it can be absolutely devoid of ingenuity, quality, or artistic value. It must, however, reflect some amount of creative effort. The alphabetized white pages of a phone book do not meet the minimum level of creativity, as was decided in 1991 with *Feist Publications v. Rural Telephone Service Company*.

The Rural Telephone Service Company had compiled a basic phone directory.

Feist wanted to compile a listing covering 11 different telephone service areas and had asked Rural for a license to use some listings from their phone book. Rural refused, Feist copied the listings anyway, and Rural sued for copyright infringement. The Supreme Court ruled that ordinary phone books were not eligible for copyright protection because the collection of facts in and of themselves was not an original creative work. Figure 11 shows the Feist Web page.

Despite the *Feist* decision, compilations are still copyrightable as long as they meet the copyright law's originality requirement. The Copyright Act defines a compilation as a "collection and assembling of preexisting materials or of data that are selected in such a way that the resulting work as a whole constitutes an original work of authorship."

For example, you could create a collage, a restaurant guide, or a Web page dedicated to your Internet radio or podcast music play

FIGURE 11
Feist Web page

lists. The list of songs in and of itself is not copyrightable, but your creative original expression of discussing, analyzing, or reviewing them is. For works such as recipes, formulas, or compounds to be eligible for copyright protection, they must have explanation or directions. Factual lists such as ingredients are not enough to meet the requirements of copyrightable expression.

QUICK**TIP**

The *Feist* case also supports telemarketers compiling calling lists from factual data, which they use to call people.

Although the Copyright Act never defines the term **work of authorship**, the Act lists categories, shown below, that exemplify the types of works that qualify. The term is deliberately broad to cover works not yet realized by new technologies.

- Literary works, such as books, poetry, plays, compilations, computer programs (including games and Web pages)
- Musical works, including lyrics or any accompanying words
- Dramatic works, including any accompanying music
- Pantomimes and choreographic works
- Pictorial, graphic, and sculptural works, including architectural plans, two- and three-dimensional art, photographs, maps, charts, diagrams, computer graphics, and models
- Motion pictures and other audiovisual works, including scores, speech, and sound effects
- Sound recordings, including music, speech, and sound not covered by motion pictures and audiovisual works
- Architectural works

Fixed in a **tangible medium of expression** refers to the form in which a work can be viewed or experienced, for no matter how brief a period of time. Examples include paper, recordings, video, digital media, or the random access memory (RAM) in a computer. The key word is tangible—talking to your dog about an idea for a movie while out on a walk and later seeing a movie made with a similar plot does not entitle you to claim copyright infringement. But, if you sent a text message detailing the screenplay (and the recipient kept the message), your expression is protected by copyright because it is fixed. You could then claim copyright infringement if someone used your script without your permission.

QUICK**TIP**

A nontangible medium of expression could be an improvisational song, dance, or speech that has not been recorded in some fashion.

What Is Not Protected?

You cannot copyright short phrases, terms, and titles, although there are exceptions. For example, a seller of coffee mugs was prohibited from using the phrase "ET phone home" on mugs because of copyright infringement because the phrase evoked the copyrighted character.

You can trademark short phrases, terms, and titles, as shown below:

- The term *Let's Roll* received a trademark after 9/11, although *Let's Roll* is also used by a rolling suitcase and backpack manufacturer.
- Fox News lost its suit against Al Franken when they claimed that he violated their trademark "fair and balanced" when he used it as parody in the title of his book, "Lies and the Lying Liars Who Tell Them: A Fair and Balanced Look at the Right."
- The Supreme Court unanimously ruled that the shop Victor's Little Secret did not infringe on the trademark held by Victoria's Secret. Legally, the name did not dilute the mark by confusing the consumer.

You can name a product such as a multimedia program the same title as another work as long as that title or name is not protected under some other type of law, such as trademark.

UNDERSTAND
Copyright Ownership

What You'll Learn

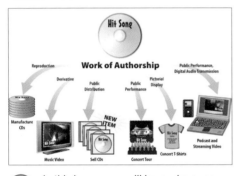

In this lesson, you will learn who owns copyright protection for a work, what exactly it is they own, and what work for hire means in copyright law.

Understanding Copyright Transfer

Usually, the owner of a copyrighted work is the author or creator of the work (or if joint authors, co-owners). A copyright owner can transfer copyright in whole or in part by license or other means. The level and scope of permissions provided in the license depend on how the work will be used, who will use the work, what geographic area it will be used in, its format, and so on. The person obtaining the license or the transfer of ownership has similar rights to the author, such as, the right to sue.

An author may contribute to a collective work, such as placing an article in a journal or an entry in an online Web log, and obtain copyright protection as soon as it is "fixed" (assuming the article meets the originality requirements). The author can transfer copyright to the publisher or can transfer only some rights, such as the right to reproduce and distribute. Once transferred, the publisher, not the author

is the copyright owner of those rights. However, if the author does not transfer copyright, the publisher only has the right to reproduce and distribute the material and only in the current collective work, not in future collections. For example, National Geographic returned copyrights for photographs taken by one of their freelance photographers, who had photographed for the magazine for over 30 years. Later, National Geographic compiled a 30-disc CD ROM library of every issue of National Geographic, including the photographer's work, and even used one of his photos on the "cover" in an animated intro. The courts ruled in favor of the photographer (and all freelancers) that his work was used improperly as part of a digital archive.

Understanding Work for Hire
The biggest exception to creator-as-author is when the creator is employed under a **work for hire** contract. In these cases, the creator is not considered the author of the work and is not entitled to

copyright protection. Hiring a photographer, writer, or graphic artist to create a product is only a work for hire arrangement when one of the following requirements is met:

- The project is a "work prepared by an employee within the scope of his or her employment."
- The project is a "work specially ordered or commissioned for use," and the contract includes specific language stating that the agreement is work for hire. (This is limited to certain types of works.)

The copyright advantage of a work for hire agreement is to the employer, plain and simple. One can always negotiate a work for hire agreement to allow the creator some rights, such as being able to use the work in their portfolio. One advantage to the creator of retaining copyright but transferring all rights to the employer or publisher is that copyright law allows the copyright to revert to the creator after 35–40 years.

What Exactly Does the Copyright Owner Own?

The Copyright Act of 1976 provided the copyright owner with a "bundle" of six rights, shown in Figure 12, and consists of:

- Reproduction
- Creation of derivative works (for example, a movie version of a book)
- Distribution to the public
- Public performance of literary, musical, dramatic, and choreographic works, pantomimes, and motion pictures and other audio-visual works
- Public display of literary, musical, dramatic, and choreographic works, pantomime, and pictorial, graphic, or sculptural works
- Public performance by digital audio transmission of sound recordings

These rights can be broken up at the discretion of the copyright holder. For example, you can grant one person the right to publicly display your digital image on a Web site, another person the right to reproduce that image in a textbook, and a third

person the right to modify the image in a graphics program.

The rights of *reproduction* and *distribution to the public* are self-explanatory, but the others can be a bit trickier.

Only a copyright holder can create a *derivative work* of their original by transforming or adapting it. For example, the film "Hairspray" has gone from movie to musical play, all under the creative guidance of its author, John Waters.

Sampling music. Modifying samples from one or more sources qualifies as a derivative work. You cannot capture the *value* of a song without permission, and the value can be as short as a 3-second snippet. For example, the immediacy with which you can recognize the opening notes of Beethoven's *Fifth Symphony*, the theme of "Jaws" by John Williams, or the introduction to Eric Clapton's "Layla" is evidence of the song's value—and all are less than six seconds in length.

Unintentionally signing away rights

When you sign a license agreement or click the "I agree" button on a Web site, you have now entered the world of contract law, where you can instantly and legally sign away your rights. Your agreement to comply with the terms set out on the site (even if you didn't really read them before you clicked "Yes, I have read and understood the terms") may prevent you from making use of your rights under copyright law. There may be restrictions on copying that negate fair uses. Even if a work is not protected, you are bound to the terms to which you agreed.

Fan fiction. The fact that some copyright owners permit fan fiction notwithstanding, the fact is writing a story using your favorite characters from a movie, book, or television show infringes on the owner's copyright. You can write about ideas and plot overviews, but not characters that are "well-developed and sufficiently delineated." Determining if characters fit that description is decided on a case-by-case basis and differentiated between cartoon characters and literary characters.

Cartoon characters that have "physical as well as conceptual qualities" are readily protected by copyright (and probably by trademark as well), while literary characters will be protected if they are so fully developed that the character stands out from the idea or plot behind the character. For example, Darth Vader, Luke Skywalker, and their neighborhood star system are not merely an emperor's enforcer who dresses in black, a young protector dressed in a white sashed shirt, and a galaxy far, far away.

Performing or displaying publicly occurs in a public place where the majority of people are strangers to you and you transmit or communicate the performance to them, wherever they may be. For example, you have publicly performed a motion picture if you upload your copyrighted short film to your Web site where it plays whenever a user clicks a button, or you take a DVD of the film to your favorite local coffee shop where the owner plays it on her plasma television.

The owner of copyright in a sound recording has a separate public performance right, but only if the performance is a digital audio transmission of the sound recording. Playing a CD on a stereo in the restaurant where you work is not a public performance because you are not transmitting; you are not sending the sounds beyond the stereo.

The Copyright Statute, which is updated periodically, stipulates the right of attribution and integrity to the author of a work of visual art. **Attribution** allows an author of a work of visual art (for example, a painting, drawing, print, or sculpture in a single copy or a limited edition) to claim authorship and prevent use of his or her name on a work he or she didn't create. **Integrity** allows an author to prevent the use of his or her name if the work is distorted, mutilated, or modified in a way that would harm the artist's honor or reputation.

FIGURE 12
Copyright owner's rights

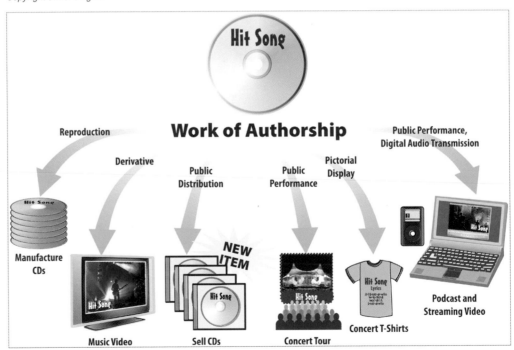

UNDERSTAND INTERNATIONAL
Copyright

What You'll Learn

▶ *In this lesson, you will learn about international copyright law and how it affects your rights and responsibilities in the United States.*

Understanding International Copyright

When working on Internet projects, you need to be aware of the international law that affects your ability to use materials and to protect your work. Web sites that originate in another country may have different limitations on use than the United States. For example, in Canada, copyright protection extends to works produced by the government. If you engage in an international lawsuit, jurisdictional issues may arise regarding the proper location for a lawsuit and the law used to decide a case.

QUICKTIP

You must also consider international treaties when using works from the Internet that may be housed on servers outside the United States.

According to the U.S. Copyright Office, "There is no such thing as an 'international copyright' that will automatically protect an author's writings throughout the world. Protection against unauthorized use in a particular country basically depends on the national laws of that country."

Fortunately, many nations are party to a host of international conventions and treaties that offer some protection to foreign works. For an updated list of countries maintaining copyright relations with the United States, visit the U.S. Copyright Office (*www.copyright.gov*) and search for Circular 38A.

The United States is signatory to two principal international copyright conventions, the Berne Convention and the Universal Copyright Convention.

Under the **Berne Convention** (which the United States did not join until 1989 because it would not amend U.S. copyright law to be in compliance), foreign authors receive the same copyright protection as the authors in a given country. This "national treatment" ensures that a U.S. author will receive the same protections in Canada that a Canadian author would receive in the U.S. The Berne Convention is shown in Figure 13.

The United States joined the **Universal Copyright Convention (UCC)** treaty in 1955. The treaty provided many of the protections of the Berne Convention, such as national treatment and a minimum copyright term equal to the life of the author plus 25 years.

Other recent treaties, such as the General Agreement on Tariffs and Trade (GATT) Trade Related Aspects of Intellectual Property (TRIPS), dealt with issues such as importing infringing goods and anticircumvention provisions.

FIGURE 13
Berne Convention

Berne Convention
for the Protection of Literary and Artistic Works

Paris Act
of July 24, 1971,
as amended on
September 28, 1979

Berne Convention
for the Protection of Literary and Artistic Works

of September 9, 1886,
completed at PARIS on May 4, 1896,
revised at BERLIN on November 13, 1908,
completed at BERNE on March 20, 1914,
revised at ROME on June 2, 1928,
at BRUSSELS on June 26, 1948,
at STOCKHOLM on July 14, 1967,
and at PARIS on July 24, 1971,
and amended on September 28, 1979

TABLE OF CONTENTS*

Article 1:   *Establishment of a Union*

Article 2:   *Protected Works:* 1. "Literary and artistic works"; 2. Possible requirement of fixation; 3. Derivative works; 4. Official texts; 5. Collections; 6. Obligation to protect; beneficiaries of protection; 7. Works of applied art and industrial designs; 8. News

Article 2bis: *Possible Limitation of Protection of Certain Works:* 1. Certain speeches; 2. Certain uses of lectures and addresses; 3. Right to make collections of such works

Article 3:   *Criteria of Eligibility for Protection:* 1. Nationality of author; place of publication of work; 2. Residence of author; 3. "Published" works; 4. "Simultaneously published" works

Article 4:   *Criteria of Eligibility for Protection of Cinematographic Works, Works of Architecture and Certain Artistic Works*

The Berne Convention is administered by WIPO, shown in Figure 14. WIPO is an agency of the United Nations responsible for protecting copyright throughout the world. WIPO's objective is the "promotion of the effective protection and use of intellectual property throughout the world through cooperation with and among Member States and all other stakeholders."

For more detailed information about international copyright protection and foreign copyright law for selected countries, review the online appendix, "International Copyright Law."

FIGURE 14
WIPO

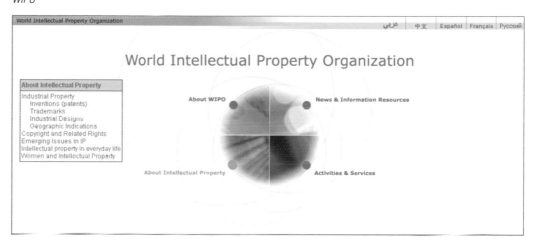

Background on the Berne Convention

In 1886, several countries formed and signed the Berne Convention for the Protection of Literary and Artistic Works. Signatories to the convention granted foreign authors the same rights as their country of origin. These rights included translations, alterations, public performances or broadcasts, and so on. Also included were **moral rights**, which encompass attribution and integrity rights. The United States did not become signatory to the Berne Convention until 1989.

UNDERSTAND HOW TO
Protect Work

What You'll Learn

▶ *In this lesson, you will learn about how to register your copyright, the advantage of registering, and digital protection technology.*

Understanding Copyright Registration

While you may not think twice about downloading work you want to use, the thought of someone using something you created and possibly profiting from it may give you pause.

Although copyright protection begins as soon as the work is created in a fixed, tangible medium, your strongest legal position is established when you officially register the work with the Copyright Office at the Library of Congress (*www.copyright.gov*). Registering your work has many advantages:

- By registering the copyright, it officially becomes part of the public record, including the date it was registered. Courts use public records to recognize the accuracy or existence of facts, in a process known as judicial notice. If the work is registered before or within five years of publication, the registration will establish *prima facie*

evidence in court of the validity of the copyright and of the facts stated in the certificate.
- Registering the copyright is required in order for the owner to file a copyright infringement suit against an alleged infringer (although only for works of U.S. origin).
- If the work is registered within three months after publication of the work or prior to an infringement of the work and the copyright owner wins a copyright infringement suit, they can be awarded statutory damages and attorneys' fees (at the discretion of the court). Otherwise, the award can only include actual damages and profits.
- Registering the work allows the copyright owner to record the registration with the U.S. Customs Service for protection against others importing pirated copies.

Registering Copyright

The Copyright Office Web site, shown in Figure 15, provides extensive information about copyright law and houses the copyright database. To research whether a work you want to use has copyright protection, you can search in three databases: books, music, and other registered works; serials; and documents. For example, if you search on the term *surf and turf* (and closely associated terms such as *surf n turf* and *surf & turf*) you will find titles of copyrighted works that include writings by a long-time writer from *The New Yorker*, a song, a screenplay, a nondramatic literary work, and a greeting card. Remember that even though you cannot copyright a title, the term is trademarked as a sound effects pedal for electric guitars and a flavor of cat food. One could safely conclude that this book title would not be confused with or take business away from any trademarked products.

Registering your copyright is straightforward: you fill out a form from the Copyright Office, submit a low fee ($30 at the time of this printing), include copies of the work for deposit, and wait for the reply (which could take several months). The registration becomes effective on the day the Copyright Office receives the package, regardless of when they send out notification. The Copyright Office has separate forms for literary works, visual arts, performing arts, sound recordings, and serials/periodicals. Figure 16 shows the registration form for visual arts.

FIGURE 15

U.S. Copyright Office Web site

FIGURE 16

Copyright form for a visual work of art

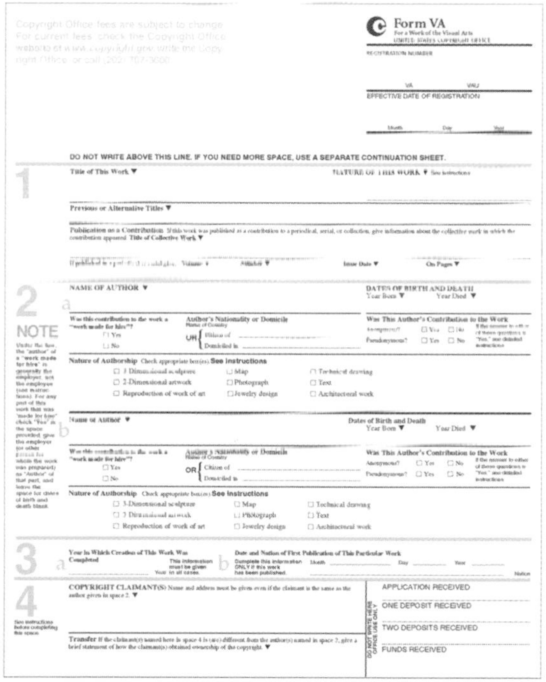

Posting a Copyright Notice

The familiar © symbol or "Copyright" is no longer required to indicate copyright, nor does it automatically register your work, but it does serve a useful purpose. When you post or publish it, you are stating clearly to those who may not know anything about copyright law that this work is claimed by you and is not in the public domain. Your case is made even stronger if someone violates your copyright and your notice is clearly visible. A violator can never claim ignorance of the law as an excuse for infringing.

The proper notification can be either:
Copyright 2006 Course Technology
or
© 2006 Course Technology

The year refers to the date the work was created; modifications made later have that year appended to the notice.

Understanding Watermarks

Watermarks were first produced in the Middle Ages during the paper-making process. Watermarks were made by a wire sewn onto the paper mold. They identified the paper maker, which attested to the product's authenticity and quality. Watermarks have also been useful in authenticating bank notes. Figure 17 shows the latest printed watermark technology applied to a $50 U.S. bank note.

FIGURE 17
Watermark in a bank note

Watermark

As computer graphics developed, it was an easy transition to create a visible watermark using image-editing tools such as Adobe Photoshop, Macromedia Fireworks, or Jasc Paint Shop Pro. Figure 18 shows a digitally produced watermark that renders the image unsuitable for unauthorized use.

While the purpose of printed and graphically created watermarks is to be visible, digital watermark technology is designed to be undetectable. Based on security algorithms, a **digital watermark** embeds a hidden code into a digital audio, video, or image file or signal. The code creates a pattern that can be a copyright notice or verification message. It serves to uniquely identify the file. If the file is suspected to have been used without permission, the code can be extracted and its download or distribution history traced to determine any unauthorized use. Figure 19 shows how a digital watermark works.

QUICKTIP

The next generation of digital watermark technology may include computer-generated holograms.

FIGURE 18

Watermark created in a graphics program

Subtle watermark created with a text tool

FIGURE 19

How a digital watermark works

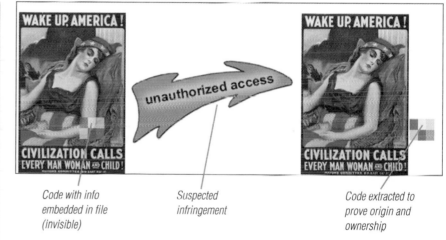

Code with info embedded in file (invisible)

Suspected infringement

Code extracted to prove origin and ownership

Match each term with the statement that best describes it.

_____ 1. Tangible medium

_____ 2. Patent

_____ 3. Broadcast flag

_____ 4. Progress Clause

_____ 5. Trade secret

_____ 6. Digital watermark

_____ 7. © 2006 Course Technology

_____ 8. Intellectual property

a. Digital code used to identify or verify a work

b. Digital code used to prevent copying

c. Examples include discoveries, performances, music, and inventions

d. Examples include audio or video tape, paper, and computer disc

e. A provision in the Constitution that authorizes copyright protection

f. Copyright notice

g. Examples include logos, formulas, and patterns

h. Exclusive rights given to an inventor

Select the best answer from the list of choices.

9. Which of the following would *not* be considered a work of authorship?

a. A birthday card you made for your mother in 1st grade

b. Your audition video for American Idol

c. A spontaneous poetry slam

d. Faces you drew of your coworkers in a staff meeting

10. What can copyright registration be used for?

a. To legally use a © symbol

b. To protect a work in a foreign country

c. To extend copyright protection

d. To sue a copyright infringer

11. Which area of intellectual property do states govern?

a. Patents

b. Right of publicity

c. Trademark™ registration

d. Copyright extensions

12. Which organization handles international copyright issues?

a. WIPO

b. CTEA

c. DMCA

d. FCC

13. Which of the following meets a requirement for a work for hire contract?

a. The work will be chosen as the winner from dozens of applicants.

b. The work is created by an independent contractor who contacted the company with an idea.

c. The work is created by compiling facts from other works.

d. The work is created by an employee whose job description includes that work.

Understand intellectual property law.

1. Using your favorite word-processing program, open a document and save it as **Copyright Analysis**.
2. Explain how intellectual property differs from real or personal property.
3. What is the difference between copyright law and patent law?
4. Save your work.

Understand the purpose of copyright.

1. Describe how different the Internet might be if HTML were always under copyright or patent protection.
2. As a musician, describe how having copyright protection of only five years would affect your ability to make a living, interest in creating more songs, interest in creating better songs, and music in general.
3. Discuss the impact the Copyright Term Extension Act had on works entering the public domain.
4. Save your work.

Understand copyright protection.

1. Discuss how society gains or loses by having long terms of copyright protection.
2. List three categories of works of authorship.
3. List three tangible media of expression.
4. Save your work.

Understand copyright ownership.

1. Discuss how the effects of removing an author's right to create derivative works would affect their revenue stream.
2. Discuss how fan fiction could limit an author's ability to create sequels or new work.
3. Save your work.

Understand international copyright.

1. Discuss what would happen if the United States did not honor international copyright treaties with countries whose citizens were considered enemies of the United States.
2. Save your work.

Understand how to protect work.

1. Discuss the advantages of registering your work with the Copyright Office.
2. Discuss the advantages of digital watermarking capable of tracking any media into which it is embedded.
3. Save your work, add your name at the top of the documents, print one copy, then close Copyright Analysis.

You occasionally freelance as a photographer for The Weekly Pulse, an alternative newspaper. They call you to photograph a subject and pay you a flat rate for each photo they use. One of your photos was selected as Best Pet Photo of the Year by the largest newspaper in your state. The photo has generated great buzz, and you've received e-mails and phone calls offering praise and congratulations. Now you've heard that a small pet clothing Web site is using your image in a collage, on their home page, though they do not specifically sell a product on that page. That was the last straw, and now you want to stop everyone from infringing on your photo.

1. Open your favorite word processor, then create a new document and save it as **Better Late Than Never** in the drive and folder where you are storing files for this book.
2. As an independent photographer, answer the following questions:
   - Were you under a work for hire contract with The Weekly Pulse?
   - What factors determine a work for hire contract? What factors make it difficult to determine if you were under a work for hire contract?
   - Can you still register your prize-winning photo? Why or why not?
3. Save your work, then close the document.

You own a home furnishing shop named Deeply Retro Repro, which specializes in 1960s and 1970s suburban furniture and art. Your ability to accessorize any interior has landed you several design awards. Now, you're concerned it might land you in jail. One of your work-for-hire assistants returned from a nationwide tour of garage sales and swap meets with a moving van full of stuff, and is now busily adding them to the company Web site. To help her understand the copyright issues involved in your work, you discuss some of her finds with her.

1. Open your favorite word processor, then start a new document and save it as **Deeply Retro Repro** in the drive and folder where you are storing files for this book.

2. Identify the copyright status of the following items and how you can use the work, if at all:

- Deeply Retro Repro welding together found objects such as auto parts and old copper Jell-O molds to make a lamp.
- A Twilight Zone lampshade. Your assistant plans to repaint parts of it to create a new color scheme.
- Large blank canvases that will be used to re-create the Old Masters in room décor colors.
- Andy Warhol prints, duplicated and resized using a large-format copy machine, and framed for resale.

3. Save your work, then close the document.

2

UNDERSTANDING
Infringement and Fair Use

1. Understand infringement.

2. Understand fair use.

3. Understand infringement legalities.

4. Understand the public domain.

chapter 2 UNDERSTANDING
Infringement and Fair Use

You can safely assume that unless specifically stated otherwise, every image and media file on the Internet has copyright protection. Copyright protection attaches to an expression of an idea as soon as the expression is fixed in a tangible medium of expression. U.S. copyright law allows for exceptions to an author's copyright, known legally as limitations. The starting point for understanding the limitations is knowing what constitutes infringement. The criteria and determinants of infringement vary depending on what type of intellectual property is in question, but the common denominator in all cases is that someone has used someone else's exclusive right to their intellectual property without permission.

In the legal world, the words *infringement* and *violation* have special meaning. In intellectual property, you can infringe someone's copyright, patent, or trademark, whereas rights of publicity and privacy are said to be *violated*. And, if you are ever sued and the court finds that you have indeed infringed or violated, you are *liable*, not guilty. It's most important that you understand the concepts behind the laws, regardless of the words you use.

In matters of copyright, infringement occurs when someone uses the copyrighted writing or media without permission or royalty payment. The foremost limitation upon, or exception to, copyright protection is fair use. Fair use permits the public to use copyrighted material for certain purposes without obtaining prior consent from the owner. There are no hard and fast rules on what will be considered fair use—the doctrine is always applied on a case-by-case basis. However, knowing how cases have been decided will provide you with some idea of what will be found to be fair use.

QUICKTIP

The fair use doctrine—that is, the legal rules and principles that comprise this concept—was codified with passage of the Copyright Act of 1976.

Once a work enters the public domain, intellectual property protections end. Factors such as copyright expiration and author's intent affect a work's passing into the public domain.

UNDERSTAND
Infringement

What You'll Learn

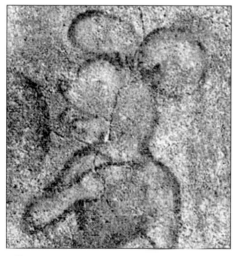

In this lesson, you will learn about copyright infringement and right of publicity violation, and you'll see how these issues play out in several case examples.

What Is Infringement?

Infringement is any unauthorized use of someone's intellectual property. Determining infringement varies depending on the type of intellectual property. Table 1 lists the rights that are infringed for a sampling of intellectual property.

Copyright Infringement

Copyright infringement is the violation of one or more of the rights granted to a copyright owner by making unauthorized use of the work. Infringement can take many forms, including:

- Making a copy of a work by downloading it to your hard drive
- Taking a photograph of a work
- Distributing copyrighted music over the Internet
- Creating a new musical work by sampling an existing work
- Building a house from a copyrighted design
- Inline linking (displaying an image from a copyrighted Web site on your Web site)

- Showing (performing) a copyrighted movie in a public place

You can also be held liable for someone else's direct infringement through your own contributory or vicarious infringement. **Contributory infringement** is conduct (yours) that assists the infringement, such as providing a product whose use is central to another person's ability to infringe. Examples include advertising to users that your software can download any music and movies for free, or distributing a product which is then "passed off" as something that is subject to trademark protection, such as selling an off-brand cola in a restaurant that has Coca-Cola signs posted. **Vicarious infringement** occurs when you have the "right and ability to supervise the infringing activity" and a financial interest in supporting that infringement. This indirect liability has come into prominence with the development of digital copying and sharing technology. Table 2 summarizes court cases that have contributed to the current legal status quo. The net result: developing technology that *could be* used to facilitate copyright infringement has been considered the same as actually infringing.

A notable exception has been **Internet Service Providers (ISPs)**. Since passage of the DMCA in 1998, ISPs are not liable for the infringing activities undertaken by their subscribers, as long as the ISP meets the safe harbor requirements of the Act, which consists of having procedures in place for receiving notices of a subscriber's infringement and for removing the infringing materials. Safe harbor for ISPs refers to the steps that ISPs can take to prevent themselves from being sued.

The Many Shades of Infringement

When deciding infringement cases, judges consider the extent of the use. **Substantial similarity**, the test for copyright infringement, looks at the degree to which a work resembles the copyrighted work. It does not have to consist of line-by-line copying.

TABLE 1: Infringing Actions

property	actions
Copyright	Reproducing, adapting, distributing, performing in public, or displaying in public the copyrighted work of someone else or transmitting digital audio without authorization
Trademark	Unauthorized use or imitation of a mark that is the property of another in order to deceive, confuse, or mislead others
Utility patent	Making, using, or selling a patented product or process without authorization
Design patent	Unauthorized fabrication of a design that, to the ordinary observer, is substantially the same as an existing design, where the resemblance is intended to induce the observer to purchase one thing supposing it to be another

TABLE 2: Digital Copying and File Sharing Decisions

year	name	technology	results of ruling
1984	*Sony Corp. of America v. Universal City Studios, Inc.*	Video recording	Taping off-air (time-shifting) for personal use does not constitute copyright infringement
2000	*A & M Records, Inc. v. Napster, Inc.*	Peer-to-peer file sharing (centralized server indexing/linking; Napster controlled database)	Technology violates rights of reproduction and distribution; Napster held liable for contributory and vicarious infringement
2005	*MGM v. Grokster*	Peer-to-peer file sharing (decentralized indexing; Grokster had no control over clients' indexing on network and could not prevent infringement)	Promoting use of software to infringe copyright is inducement; software developers violate copyright by providing users with the means to share downloaded music and movie files

Substantial similarity is easily applicable to musical compositions, and in sometimes unexpected ways. For example, in 1976, George Harrison was sued for infringement of The Chiffons' song "He's So Fine" with his song "My Sweet Lord." "He's So Fine" was readily available to the public as a hit pop song playing on the radio in 1963, when Harrison was gaining fame with The Beatles. The two songs were analyzed for similarity by experts who identified two motifs that were repeated in both songs. The court held that this constituted substantial similarity, so Harrison was guilty of infringement. However, Harrison's degree of culpability was softened by the ruling's use of the term "subconscious" copying. You can compare the two songs by connecting to the Internet, navigating to the Online Companion for this book, and then clicking Link 1. Click the Play button to listen to the songs, as shown in Figure 1.

In another case, the court ruled that a claim can be dismissed if the use is considered *de minimis*; that is, the copying lacks significance or is so minor that there are no grounds for infringement. The test is when an average audience would not recognize the appropriation. In 2003 the Beastie Boys were exonerated from infringing on James Newton's jazz work because they sampled three notes from his song "Choir" in the beginning of their song "Pass the Mic." You can compare the two songs by connecting to the Internet, navigating to the Online Companion of this book, and

FIGURE 1
Comparing George Harrison and The Chiffons

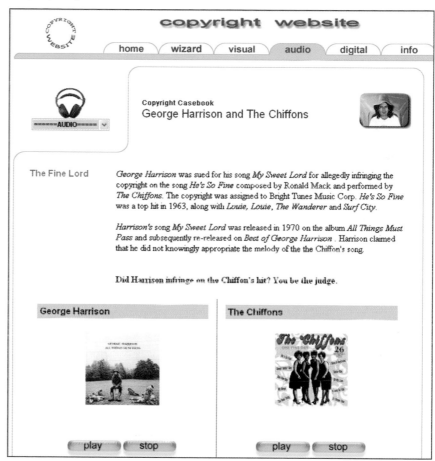

clicking Link 2. Scroll down to 2001-2010, click **Newton v. Diamond**, then click the Hear Sound Recording link to listen to the songs, as shown in Figure 2.

QUICK**TIP**

A legal gray area exists for technology such as BitTorrent, which has no search utility for locating files and clearly warns users that they are legally responsible for their actions. However, federal authorities (Homeland Security) shut down Elite Torrents network users after thousands downloaded the prerelease of *Star Wars: Episode III.*

Derivative Works: A Difficult Balance of Rights

Derivative works are those which involve adapting, recasting, or transforming one or more preexisting works. The right to create derivative works helps sustain motivation for artists and authors to create the original works. The balance between preserving the rights of the copyright owner to exploit their work financially and the right of the new author or artist to build upon it is an uneasy one.

Consider the case of Ferdinand Pickett, a guitar maker, and the artist formerly known as... the Artist Formerly Known as Prince. In 1993, Ferdinand Pickett created a guitar that was shaped like the symbol for the artist formerly known as Prince. Pickett showed the guitar to Prince, who shortly thereafter had a guitar made by someone else with a similar shape. Pickett sued Prince for infringement and Prince countersued based on Pickett's unauthorized use of Prince's copyrighted symbol.

FIGURE 2

Comparing Newton and the Beastie Boys

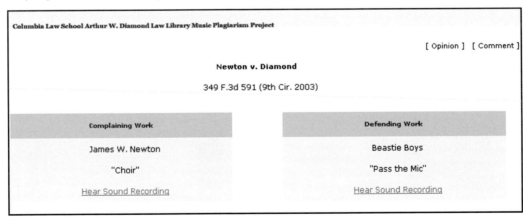

Columbia Law School Arthur W. Diamond Law Library Music Plagiarism Project

[Opinion] [Comment]

Newton v. Diamond

349 F.3d 591 (9th Cir. 2003)

Complaining Work	Defending Work
James W. Newton	Beastie Boys
"Choir"	"Pass the Mic"
Hear Sound Recording	Hear Sound Recording

Result: The court found in Prince's favor, holding that the guitar designer could not create a derivative work based on Prince's symbol without Prince's permission.

Internet Innovations and Copyright Law

Not surprisingly, Internet-specific cases have introduced new concepts that have reshaped copyright law. For example:

- In 1993, Ticketmaster lost a suit against Tickets.com who had initiated the practice of deep linking directly to a Ticketmaster page, bypassing Ticketmaster's home page and all the ensuing advertising between the home page and the concert ticket page. **Result:** The court held that "hyperlinking does not itself involve a violation of the Copyright Act—since no copying is involved. The customer is automatically transferred to the particular genuine Web page of the original author."

QUICK**TIP**

Currently, Tickets.com and Ticketmaster sell their own tickets, although not necessarily for the same dates, and both sites omit smaller concert venues.

- In 1999, photographer Leslie Kelly sued Arriba Soft Corporation because Arriba had posted thumbnails that users could click to view a larger version on Kelly's Web site.

Result: Displaying the thumbnails was fair use; inline linking to Kelly's Web site was copyright infringement. Figure 3 shows current use of thumbnails on Ditto.com, a visual search engine site.

FIGURE 3
Ditto.com Web site

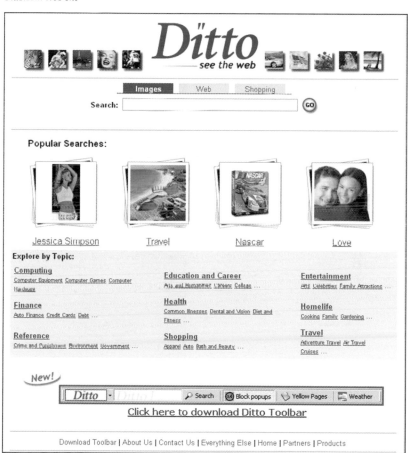

Copyright protection exists and can be pursued through legal action no matter how integrated a work is in society.

- The song "Happy Birthday" was originally written by sisters Mildred and Patty Hill, copyrighted in 1935, and with the provisions of the CTEA, will not enter the public domain until 2030. The copyright is now owned by AOL Time Warner and licensed and enforced by the American Society of Composers, Authors, and Publishers (ASCAP). In the mid-1990s, ASCAP informed the Girl Scouts that they must pay license fees to use any of the four million copyrighted songs written or published by ASCAP's 68,000 members, including "Happy Birthday" and a host of folk songs, such as "Puff the Magic Dragon."

Result: Girl Scouts eventually paid a nominal licensing fee of $1 for "Happy Birthday," but the status of other organizations is uncertain. What is certain is that a movie or television producer pays royalties anytime "Happy Birthday" is sung on-screen. Figure 4 shows the Web page for Warner Chappell, the music division of AOL Time Warner. You can search for licensed versions of copyrighted songs, such as Marilyn Monroe's version of "Happy Birthday" sung to President Kennedy in 1962. To listen to this version, connect to the Internet, navigate to the Online Companion of this book, and click Link 3. Click the Begins With list arrow, click Exact, click the Enter Keywords text box, type Happy Birthday to You, then click Search. Click the sound icon on the line with Mildred J. Hill, Patty S. Hill as the writers. You may need to first download the player.

QUICKTIP

Royalties for "Happy Birthday" bring in over $2 million annually.

- In 1989, the Walt Disney Company discovered that three Florida daycare centers had painted large images of Mickey, Minnie, and Goofy on its walls.

FIGURE 4
Marilyn Monroe's licensed version of Happy Birthday

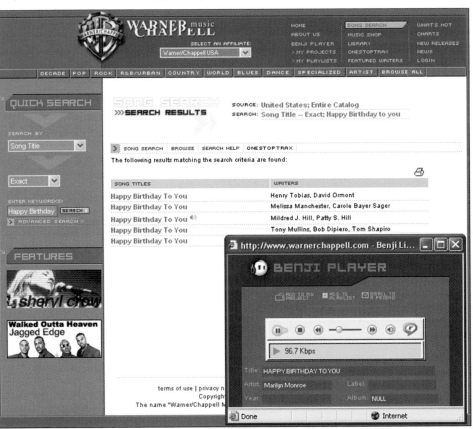

Disney threatened legal action if the centers did not paint over the images because the centers clearly violated Disney's copyright and trademarks. **Result:** Upon hearing of the incident, representatives from rivals Hanna-Barbera and Universal Studios painted over the walls with images of Yogi

Bear, Fred Flintstone, and Scooby Doo free of charge and rededicated the murals in a media event.

Interestingly, in 2002, a medieval fresco was uncovered in the Austrian village of Malta that appears to show a 700-year-old image of Mickey Mouse, shown in Figure 5. The village has (jokingly) claimed copyright infringement by Disney.

Right of Publicity and Privacy Infringement

Right of publicity is the right to protect your identity from use by others for commercial purposes, a right most frequently asserted by celebrities. Generally, a celebrity is someone who is widely recognized in society due to an accomplishment, which in the United States can range from winning sports events like Serena Williams, being a successful actor like Matt Damon, or simply being born the great grandchild of a self-made billionaire, as is Paris Hilton. Violating the right of publicity occurs when someone appropriates a celebrity's identity to promote products or other commercial ventures. Only the celebrity has exclusive rights to commercially exploit their identity. An identity is defined as their name, voice, and likeness.

A right of privacy infringement is the unwarranted public disclosure of someone's private life.

Rights of publicity and privacy started as common law (law made from legal decisions, not legislative action), but are now statutory rights in some states. The rights protected vary from state to state.

FIGURE 5
Alleged "original" Mickey Mouse on Austrian fresco

"This Land" becomes no man's land

Among the songs in ASCAP's collection is Woody Guthrie's "This Land Is Your Land," a perennial campfire chestnut. The song gained notoriety in the 2004 Presidential campaign after the Web animation site Jib Jab produced "This Land," a political parody. Ludlow Music, who thought they held the copyright to "This Land is Your Land," threatened to sue Jib Jab, contending that the work offered no "satirical comment" on the Guthrie original. It turned out Ludlow did not own rights to the song.

Right of publicity claims are often paired with the Lanham Act, a federal statute passed in 1946 that established procedures for protecting people against unfair competition, including prohibition against trying to confuse the public into thinking that your product is the product of a (commercially known) third party.

Avatars are commonplace in Internet forums, instant messaging, and games. An **avatar** is a graphical image of a person, such as a photograph, that represents the person speaking or playing. Although many images are no doubt used without permission, avatar users have not been charged with violation of publicity because they are seen as benign or helpful to a celebrity's promotion, and users derive no financial gain from their use. Figure 6 shows sample celebrity avatars.

Right of Publicity Violations

Many celebrities have successfully sued to protect their rights of publicity, as described in the cases below.

- Advertisers for Ford Motor Company and Frito Lay separately approached Bette Midler and Tom Waits, respectively, to sing in ads promoting a car and Doritos. Both declined and in each instance the advertiser hired impersonators to sing instead. In Midler's case, they hired one of her backup singers to sing one of her songs, while the Waits impersonator sang an original tune.

Result: Both artists received financial damages and the cases firmly established that voice can be as significant an identifier as name or likeness.

Evoking a celebrity's likeness is a violation, even if there is no direct attempt at imitation.

- *White v. Samsung Electronics America* challenged Samsung's use of a robot, presumably evoking Vanna White, in an ad set in the future on a Wheel of Fortune set. The robot turned letters,

as White has done for years on the game show.
Result: White received damages as the court ruled that evoking a celebrity's image in the public mind is the same as using an element of their identity.

Not surprisingly, California, New York, and Tennessee passed the most far-reaching legislation defining and protecting these rights. For example, the estate of Elvis Presley Enterprises, a for-profit business

FIGURE 6
Sample celebrity avatars

co-owned by heir Lisa Marie and a business partner, controls Graceland and all the Elvis merchandising and licensing of his image and songs. Elvis impersonators (and other celebrity impersonators) exercise their free speech through their impersonation—as long as they do not sell merchandise with Elvis' name instead of their own.

Nonviolations of Rights of Publicity

A celebrity's identity is not sacrosanct. There are certain conditions under which using an image is proper and protected speech, as you will learn about more in the next lesson. For example:

- After Schwarzenegger's election as California governor, the Bosley Bobbers Fun Products Company added to their existing bobblehead line a bobblehead of Arnold Schwarzenegger

accessorized with an assault rifle and bandolier, shown in Figure 7. Schwarzenegger claimed the doll violated his right of publicity; the company claimed that he no longer had that protection because he was now an elected official whose likeness is in the public domain.

FIGURE 7
Schwarzenegger bobblehead

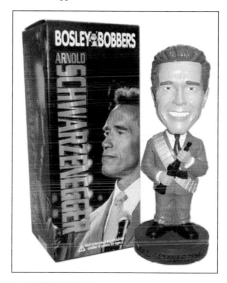

Result: The parties settled with these terms: Bosley Bobbers has the right to sell the bobblehead, but created a new one sans rifle, and donated a portion of their profits to a Schwarzenegger charity and to a charity of their choice.

Paparazzi and rights of publicity and privacy

Violating the right of publicity involves commercial gain to the violator, which at first may clearly seem to include paparazzi. Even though they sell their photographs for profit, paparazzi are not viewed as promoting a product, so their behavior does not violate a celebrity's right of publicity. Paparazzi behavior, of course, is subject to harassment and stalking laws. The right of privacy for public figures is generally limited to private spaces, such as their home, or a place where they would have a reasonable expectation of privacy, such as a hotel room, but not the hotel restaurant.

- Tiger Woods alleged his right of publicity was violated when sports artist Rick Rush painted Woods in several golf poses during his win in the 1997 U.S. Open.
  Result: The court ruled that the print was protected by the First Amendment, as the artist was conveying his unique expression of an idea (Woods' winning performance in the U.S. Open).
- Fred Astaire granted a dance studio use of his image for dance studio and related activities. As technology advanced, the dance studio commissioned videotapes, two of which featured 90 seconds of footage from Astaire movies. After his death, his widow, Robyn, sued the video production company claiming that her permission was required to show Astaire's image on the videos.
  Result: The court ruled that use of the film clips did not infringe on Robyn Astaire's widow rights.

Robyn Astaire's control of her husband's image extended to his famous former dance partner, Ginger Rogers. Fred Astaire received a Kennedy Center Honor in 1978, and Ginger Rogers allowed Astaire to show film clips of their famous dance routines during the ceremony. Astaire died in 1987. In 1992, Rogers received a Kennedy Center Honor, but Mrs. Astaire charged Ginger Rogers $150,000 per minute of screen time to show dance scenes between Rogers and Astaire. Rogers declined her offer. Mrs.

Astaire also impeded Astaire's daughter from using film clips for a tribute to her father. Mrs. Astaire did, however, sell his image to the Dirt Devil company for an ad in 1996 in which Astaire is shown dancing with a vacuum cleaner. An image of Fred Astaire from the famous "dancing on the ceiling" scene in the 1951 film *Royal Wedding* is shown in Figure 8. The film is in the public domain, so using it here does not infringe anyone's copyright. However, using the image of Astaire may violate his estate's right of publicity to his image.

Depending on the state, the right of publicity may extend beyond death. For example, California and Tennessee recognize this right but New York does not. Thus, something may enter the public domain for copyright purposes, but its use still may be protected by right of publicity or trademark.

QUICKTIP

The then cutting-edge technology that showed Astaire dance up the walls to the ceiling in 1951 was later modified for use in *2001: A Space Odyssey* and in a Lionel Ritchie music video.

FIGURE 8
Fred Astaire

UNDERSTAND
Fair Use

What You'll Learn

 In this lesson, you will learn about the factors comprising the fair use doctrine and examine several case examples.

The Fair Use Doctrine

Copyright owners are guaranteed exclusive rights to their work, but copyright law places some limitations on those rights. Understanding the fair use doctrine is essential for determining whether you can legally use copyrighted material you find on the Internet. The Copyright Act of 1976 codified the fair use doctrine that had been developing in case law for more than a century.

Fair use may be claimed when you use a portion of a copyrighted work for certain purposes without permission from the owner. It represents an excellent example of the balance between the rights of society to use creations for progress and the rights of the creators to benefit from their work.

> **QUICKTIP**
> The United Kingdom and Canada use the term *fair dealing* instead of *fair use.*

If you use even a portion of copyrighted material—for purposes such as copying text or scanning pictures from postcards, magazines, books, or any other work—and your use is not considered fair use, (or doesn't fit within another limitation on the copyright owner's rights), you have infringed the author's copyright.

The fair use doctrine identifies four factors to include when considering whether a use is fair. Of course, a decision on fair use is dependent on the specific facts of the situation—and there is no set formula that stipulates how much of any work you can use—but the breakdown helps clarify the concepts. These factors are:

Factor 1: The purpose and character of the use
- Commentary and criticism (scholarship and parody)
- News reporting
- Research
- Nonprofit versus commercial use

Factor 2: The nature of the copyrighted work
- Primarily factual versus creative
- Published versus unpublished work

Factor 3: The amount and substantiality of the portion used in relation to the copyrighted work as a whole
- Qualitative "heart of the work"
- Quantitative (the less the better)

Factor 4: The effect of the use on the market or the potential market for the copyrighted work

Under Factor 1, it makes sense not to depend on the copyright owner's permission if your intent is to criticize or comment on the work or create a parody of it. For example, the companies or people who have been parodied in *The Daily Show* skits would probably not ever give permission for such. But because these parodies are satirical—that is, they comment on or ridicule social, political, or moral principles—they are not considered infringement. Of course, to qualify as parody, the work must be satirical. A use would not qualify as a parody if the purpose is simply to get attention or avoid the time and effort necessary to create something original.

News reporting, education, scholarship, and research are examples of fair use. For example, as a film aficionado, you may want to compare clips from Alfred Hitchcock and Martin Scorsese films to analyze their artistic use of lighting and camera angles. Students and teachers need to know that even though the use may be educational, it may still violate copyright. Conversely, the fact that a work is commercial does not mean its use is not a fair use.

The role each factor plays in a decision regarding fair use varies depending on each individual situation. For example, say you want to create a Flash presentation as your final project for a contemporary and postmodern art class. You want to include as many examples as possible from smaller collections and museums, but many of them do not include any copyright or usage information. Would your Flash presentation constitute fair use or infringement? To answer the question, you must consider the four factors of fair use in weighing whether your use is fair.

Under the first factor, your use is not commercial, it is strictly nonprofit educational, which weighs toward fair use. However, this factor is also looked at as requiring the use to be transformative, rather than simply repeating the original work. **Transformative** use refers to the alteration of a work by intangible input. That is, you have achieved, in the words of one judge, a "creative metamorphosis" by adding something new, such as a new meaning or message. You could make the argument that your educational use is transformative because you are adding to the value of the work by offering new insight and interpretation through your presentation. The first factor weighs in favor of your use being a fair use.

The second factor looks at whether the work is a factual work, like a database that maps the number of bald eagle nests in Great Lakes states, or a creative one, like an animated film featuring bald eagle characters that live in Great Lakes states. An expression of fact may have "thin" copyright unless the expression is extremely creative. The facts themselves cannot be copyrighted because they are like ideas—discoverable but not protectable by copyright. So for this factor, scientific work that is highly factual with tables and limited creative expression will have less protection in its expression than will a Michael Crichton novel that uses the same scientific facts in a creative way. The second factor weighs against a fair use of the images of the art works in the Flash presentation because art works are generally considered creative rather than factual.

The third factor looks at the amount of the work you intend to copy or use in some other way that would infringe the copyright owner's rights. In your Flash presentation, you plan to use the entire image of each painting, thereby copying the totality of each work. This factor would weigh against fair use. Note that the courts do not care if you only used 10 percent of a work, or 17 images out of 100. The amount that you *didn't* use is not a defense, as the courts have consistently held that "you cannot escape liability by showing how much of [a] work you did not take."

However, it's important to note that quantity is not always the most important element when considering this factor. Using a major qualitative portion—that is, a "substantiality"—determines infringement even if you've only copied a small portion of the work. For example, in 1985, former President Gerald Ford arranged for *Harper & Row* to publish his memoirs, which then negotiated a contract with *Time* magazine to publish a 7500 word excerpt. However, *Nation* magazine scooped *Time* and printed a small excerpt (2250 words) of the memoirs before the book was released. But, what

they printed was the portion where Ford discussed his pardon of Richard Nixon, a memorable event of great interest to the public at that time because Nixon had been impeached and forced to resign from office. While other parts of the book were likely very interesting to the public, the court held that, even though the magazine only took a small part of the total work, this part was the "heart of the work." Depending on the work, the third factor regards the qualitative aspect of the portion over the amount you take from the whole. In the Flash presentation, you plan on using all of a number of works, which does not favor fair use.

The final factor examines the market for the new work. The courts have tended to focus on this factor by assessing the impact

of the new work on the market of the copyrighted work. It is weighted the most of the four factors. If the work has any effect on the market for the copyrighted work—beneficial or adverse—this factor weighs against fair use. Also included in the assessment are potential markets for the original work and its derivatives. Derivative works of a painting might include digital images such as the ones you want to use in the Flash presentation, as well as printed note cards, posters, t-shirts, shower curtains, and so on. Will your use of the image in your Flash presentation affect any of those potential markets? Probably not. This factor likely goes in your favor.

Understanding fan fiction

Fan fiction consists of stories written by enthusiastic followers and devotees of a film, television show, or other work of fiction using the characters, setting, storylines, and so on of the original. Fan fiction obviously constitutes infringement and may be legally actionable *unless* the author grants permission for the use. Despite its range of topics (and ratings), most fan fiction is pastiche. Copyright owners, whether the creator, such as J.K. Rowling (Harry Potter) or a company, such as Paramount Pictures (*Star Trek*), may tolerate or even encourage fan fiction, as both Ms. Rowling and Paramount do. Others, such as Anne Rice (*Interview with the Vampire*) expressly forbid fan fiction and enforce their copyright protections to the fullest. The argument for fan fiction is that it takes nothing from and freely promotes the original and is not written for profit. The argument against is that it dilutes the value of the copyright.

Figure 9 summarizes how the factors weigh in for and against you when deciding whether to create your Flash presentation. Of course, although anyone can analyze the factors in a given situation, the ultimate determination rests with the court if a copyright owner decides to sue for infringement.

Personal Responsibilities

It's tempting to think that every personal use of a copyrighted work is a fair use because your arguments for using it outweigh the arguments against. For example, posting photos from your favorite television comedy shows on your Web site is infringement. However, posting those same photos on a site as part of an analysis of formulaic sitcom structure could be fair use.

Educational Responsibilities

Educational uses do allow more leeway for use. However, bear in mind that even if you can prove fair use when using someone's work for educational purposes, you still may run afoul of the educator's sense of propriety if you fail to credit your source by naming the author of the work on the same page. The same holds true when you paraphrase an author's original work on

FIGURE 9
Weighing factors for fair use

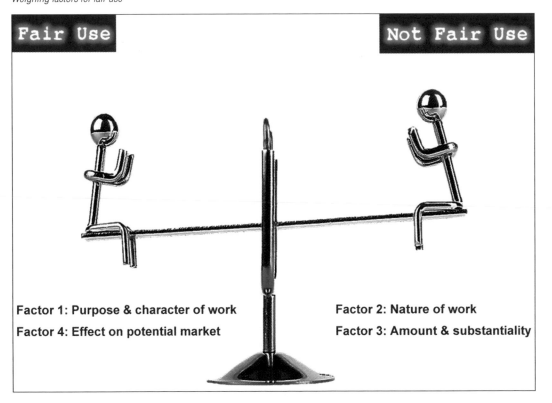

Fair Use   Not Fair Use

Factor 1: Purpose & character of work
Factor 4: Effect on potential market
Factor 2: Nature of work
Factor 3: Amount & substantiality

your Web page, term paper, and so on. If you do not credit your source, you are guilty of plagiarism. And, pattern-recognition technology has spawned companies that can check for lifted material when instructors submit students' work online, as shown in Figure 10.

QUICK**TIP**

For the proper citation of online materials, visit the University of Maryland's reference page at www.umuc.edu/ugp/ewp/citing_web.html.

When the 1976 Act was passed, educators and publishers sat down and negotiated the Classroom Guidelines (also known as the CONTU guidelines). These guidelines specify that copying for classroom use should meet the criteria of brevity, spontaneity, and lack of cumulative effect. That is, due to the nature of teaching, the teacher does not copy a significant amount, does not have the time to plan ahead and seek permissions to use the work, and does not

use the same materials over and over (same class year after year).

The Conference on Fair Use (CONFU), which issued its final report in 1998, proposed *safe harbor* guidelines for instructors and students who want to digitize analog images or to create multimedia work for class room use, self-study, or remote instruction. These are proposed guidelines only, and provide limits on quantities. For example, only 10% or

FIGURE 10
Plagiarism detection companies

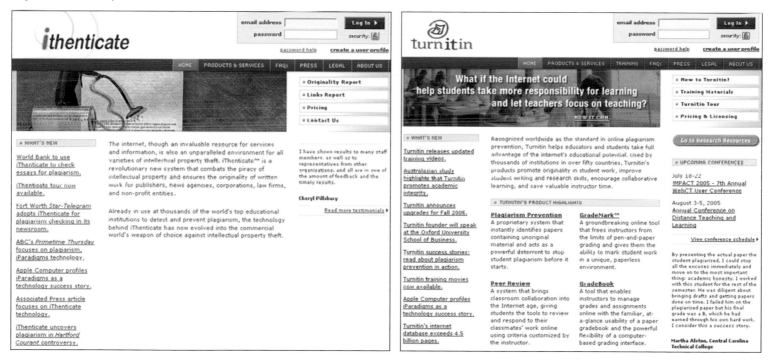

1000 words of a copyrighted text, up to 10% but not more than 30 seconds of a musical work, 10% or three minutes of a motion picture, an entire photograph but no more than five images by the same creator, or up to 10% or 2500 fields from a database. These proposed guidelines have not been embraced and incorporated into the legislative materials as the CONTU guidelines were, and, again, these are only proposed minimums; fair use analysis may provide the right to use more of a work. But the most important aspect to remember is that there is no accepted formula for using parts or percentages of any work.

In any event, even if you believe that your use is a fair use, the author may disagree and your belief could be put to an expensive legal test. Therefore, it is always safer to take the time and effort to contact the owner and request permission to use the owner's work.

Trademark Fair Use

Trademark infringement occurs when someone other than the trademark owner creates a trademark that is likely to be confused with the existing one. Factors involved in determining whether confusion exists include but are not limited to:

- Strength of the mark
- Similarity
- Intent
- Actual confusion

Trademarks have their own fair use guidelines. These include: nominative (using someone else's trademark as part of your advertising), comparative (comparing your product with another's), and parody.

The Strongest Trademark that Almost Wasn't

In 1898 British painter Francis Barraud painted his dog, Nipper, listening with rapt attention to the latest entertainment technology, the gramophone. Barraud is shown painting "His Master's Voice" in Figure 11.

Barraud tried reproducing the work in magazines but was turned down because "no one would know what the dog was doing," the gramophone being so new.

FIGURE 11
Barraud painting "His Master's Voice"

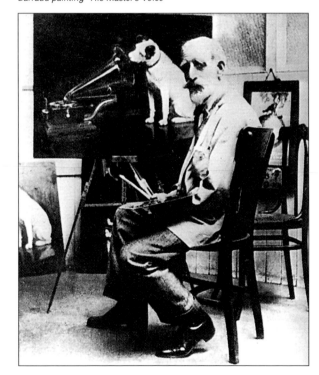

He next tried to sell it to The Edison Bell Company, U.S. patent holder and leading manufacturer of the cylinder phonograph, but was told "dogs don't listen to phonographs."

Finally, in 1899, the Gramophone Company, later the Victor Talking Machine Company, bought the U.S. rights to the painting and made the image into its trademark. The trademark transitioned after the Radio Corporation of America (RCA) bought Victor in 1920s. Barraud was paid £50 ($250) for the painting and another £50 for the copyright. "His Master's Voice" became one of the top 10 famous brands of the 20th century. Nipper was joined by a puppy, Chipper, when RCA introduced their digital line of products.

QUICK**TIP**

RCA had tremendous success in the early 20th century with the manufacturing of radios, televisions, and 45 rpm records. It later declined with less successful ventures including the eight-track tape cartridge. General Electric bought and dismantled the company in 1986.

Exploring Important Court Cases

Fair use law continues to evolve as new cases come before the courts. The following examples illustrate how popular culture and shifting societal norms continue to shape the law every day:

- In 1994, rap group 2 Live Crew recorded Roy Orbison's "Pretty Woman," the rights to which were owned by Acuff-Rose Music. While the music was easily recognizable, the group changed the lyrics. The music company sued for copyright infringement.

Cybersquatting

Cybersquatting is the act of registering a domain name with the intention of directing a searcher to the site for commercial gain. This can also be a trademark violation, especially for a celebrity, but court decisions have been mixed. For example, Julia Roberts and the estate of Jimi Hendrix have each won their arguments, while Bruce Springsteen has not.

Result: The U.S. Supreme Court found that parody weighed heavily when considering the amount of copying and the commercial nature of the work. The case established parody as fair use. You can compare the two songs by connecting to the Internet, navigating to the Online Companion of this book, and opening Link 2. Scroll down to 1990-2000, click **Acuff-Rose v. Campbell**, then click the Hear Sound Recording link to listen to the songs. Sample lyrics from both songs are shown in Figure 12.

- "The Wind Done Gone" is a retelling of the Civil War and Reconstruction as a parody from a slave's point of view (who was Scarlet O'Hara's half-sister) in the same time frame and locale in which "Gone With The Wind" was set. In 2001, the book was in the midst of being printed when the estate of "Gone With The Wind" author Margaret Mitchell sued author Alice Randall and her publisher for copyright infringement.

Result: The suit was dropped in 2002 when the publisher, Houghton Mifflin, made an undisclosed donation to Morehouse College in Atlanta, Georgia, a college for which the Mitchell estate had long been a supporter.

- Kinko's was sued by Basic Books for making and selling course packets that included excerpts and chapters from copyrighted books. Kinko's claimed that it was educational fair use.

FIGURE 12

Comparing Orbison and 2 Live Crew

Columbia Law School Arthur W. Diamond Law Library Music Plagiarism Project

[Opinion] [Comment]

Campbell v. Acuff-Rose

510 U.S. 569 (1994)

Complaining Work	Defending Work
Williams Dees and Roy Orbison	Luther Campbell et. al.
"Oh, Pretty Woman"	"Oh, Pretty Woman"
Hear Sound Recording	Hear Sound Recording
Hear MIDI file	
View Video Clip	
View Partial Score	

Pretty woman, won't you pardon me
Pretty woman, I couldn't help but see
Pretty woman, and you look lovely
  as can be
Are you lonely just like me

Big hairy woman, you need to
  shave that stuff,
Big hairy woman, you know
  I bet it's tough.
Big hairy woman, all that hair
  ain't legit,
'Cause you look like Cousin It

Result: The court held that this was not a fair use, looking closely at Kinko's commercial purpose in copying the materials and the fact that they made multiple copies. Kinko's had "extinguished" a financial reward to the copyright holder (Basic Books), which was precisely what copyright law was designed to protect.

The Kinko's and similar cases have had a very strong impact on copy shops' willingness to copy material without permission. Today, copyright information is available on the business' Web site. Sample course packs from University Readers (*www. universityreaders.com*), a reputable custom publishing and copyright clearance management company, are shown in Figure 13. The trepidation has also spilled over to digital photo processors at drug stores, who, perhaps unfamiliar with the image-editing tools available in applications such as Adobe Photoshop, refuse to print hard copies of digital photos if they look "too good."

- Toy manufacturer Mattel, maker of Barbie, has taken action numerous times to protect its trademark. In 1997, the company sued the Danish pop

FIGURE 13
Coursepacks

group Aqua for its song "Barbie Girl," claiming the group defamed Barbie by referring to her as a "blonde bimbo." Partial lyrics are shown in Figure 14. In 1999, Mattel sued artist Tom Forsythe, who photographed posed dolls in

kitchen appliances and cookware, and in 2004 Mattel sued the Quebec barbeque restaurant chain Barbie's, alleging that customers would associate it with the doll.

Result: The Supreme Court found the song and the art to be well within the realm of parody and satire. The restaurant case went to the Supreme Court of Canada. For their judgment, visit *www.scc-csc.gc.ca*.

FIGURE 14
Lyrics to Aqua's Barbie Girl

Barbie Girl Lyrics

Hi Barbie
Hi Ken!
Do you wanna go for a ride?
Sure Ken!
Jump In...

I'm a barbie girl, in a barbie world
Life in plastic, it's fantastic!

Imagination, life is your creation
Come on Barbie, let's go party!
I'm a blond bimbo girl, in a fantasy world

Understanding Infringement and Fair Use   Chapter 2

■ Photographer Art Rogers took a photograph of a couple holding six puppies, which he subsequently made into a note card. Another artist, Jeff Koons, purchased the note card, allegedly tore off the copyright notice, and sent it to an Italian forge studio with instructions to make four large sculptures using the photograph as a model. He sold the sculptures for more than $350,000. Koons never denied copying the photograph; his argument for use was based on parody and fair use, which he said was commentary on a materialistic society.

Result: The court rejected his arguments because the new work was only in a new medium which was not transformative and did not proffer parody. Using someone's copyrighted work requires permission from the owner.

Tattoos and copyright

While on the surface tattoos may seem like a straight-forward expression of an idea easily embraced by copyright law, in reality tattoos have had a distinctive relationship with the legal system and between tattoo artists. Traditionally, tattoo artists have been leery of the legal system and have not undertaken suing for copyright infringement as a remedy. Likewise, the entertainment industry and other companies have not pursued copyright infringement against artists who routinely ink popular culture icons and even company logos. Modifying and even copying designs is an accepted practice, although lately some artists have sought to assert their intellectual property rights. Artists negotiate works for hire with clients so they maintain use of the design and send cease and desist letters to authors who improperly use photographs of tattoos. One artist applied for and received a service mark trademark for a distinctive tattoo, which has deterred others using a photograph of the image to promote their tattoo or piercing business.

UNDERSTAND INFRINGEMENT
Legalities

▶ *In this lesson, you will learn about the elements and conditions that make up copyright infringement lawsuits.*

Understanding the Legal Setting for Infringement Suits

Copyright infringement cases are, for the most part, based on civil law, not criminal law. The distinction between the two is significant. The assumptions and burdens of proof governing copyright infringement are less rigorous in civil law than they would be in criminal law. In civil law, there is never the need to show infringement beyond a reasonable doubt, and there may even be an assumption of "guilt"—responsibility. In a copyright infringement case, once the copyright owner has met the burden of establishing a *prima facie* case of infringement (alleged evidence sufficient to prove a case), the burden shifts onto the alleged infringer to prove that he or she did not infringe. For example, U.S. copyright law specifically prohibits removing a watermark from a photograph. If you are sued for removing a watermark, the attempt itself is viewed by the court as evidence of your intent to violate the owner's copyright. The assumption is that you are liable and you must prove that you're not. It is a stark contrast to criminal law, where the defendant in a criminal matter is presumed innocent until proven guilty, and the burden is on the prosecution to prove guilt beyond a reasonable doubt.

What Must Be Proven to Make a Case?

In a civil copyright infringement case, the copyright owner must establish infringement by proving the elements described below:

- The work is protected by copyright (and registered with the Copyright Office).
- The infringer has copied the work, as shown by:
  - the infringer's admission (rare, but it happens) *or*
  - the copyright owner offering circumstantial evidence of infringing by demonstrating that the alleged infringer had access to the work and that the alleged infringing work was substantially similar to the copyrighted work.

- The use of the work was improper. You have to prove that not only did the person copy your work (as opposed to copying someone else's work or independently creating it), but they also took the protected expression from your copyrighted work. The test for improper use may be verbatim copying of the whole work (a reproduction) or of a part of the work (sampling), or the infringer may have copied the "total concept and feel" of your work (for example, a character so closely resembles your character that the ordinary observer would think they were similar).

The copying must be proved to be substantially taken from protectable work and also used improperly.

Chilling Effects: Where Politics Meets Reality

In 2003, the Recording Industry Association of America (RIAA) began suing individuals for illegally distributing copyrighted music files downloaded from P2P networks. In music file sharing and other infringement cases, the threat of legal action is often as effective as initiating legal action (and cheaper, too). The first people the RIAA went after for illegal downloads were middle and high school students, some of whom wound up paying $12,000 in damages (the students themselves, not their parents). Of course, the families could have tried to negotiate a better settlement or hired an attorney, but that also costs money and time. The entertainment industry has extensive resources that can be brought to bear in long, complex, and expensive cases. Defendants, especially individual consumers or fledgling artists, may not have the financial resources to defend themselves in kind.

Tom Forsythe, an artist who was sued by Mattel after using Barbie dolls in a photographic social commentary, is a rare case. After five years and numerous appeals, Mr. Forsythe was found not to have infringed Mattel's trademark and was awarded costs for his legal fees: $1.8 million. In that ruling the judge stated that "(p)laintiff (Mattel) had access to sophisticated counsel who could have determined that such a suit was objectively unreasonable and frivolous. Instead it appears plaintiff forced defendant into costly litigation to discourage him from using Barbie's image in his artwork. This is just the sort of situation in which this court should award attorneys fees to deter this type of litigation which contravenes the intent of the Copyright Act." It should be noted that after Mattel first filed suit in 1999, Mr. Forsythe had difficulty obtaining counsel until the American Civil Liberties Union of Southern California and a San Francisco law firm agreed to take his case.

Mattel also challenged Forsythe's nominative use of Barbie dolls in their suit (the number of Barbies used); they lost on this count, as well.

For many companies, lawsuits against less powerful infringers serve as a chilling effect on future offenders. For additional information on when certain actions are intended to limit online speech or expression, visit the Chilling Effects Clearinghouse, shown in Figure 15. The organization "aims to support lawful online activity against the chill of unwarranted legal threats."

What Will Happen if You Infringe Copyright

If you use someone's copyrighted work without permission, you likely will first receive a cease-and-desist letter (discussed in Chapter 4). If you believe that your use is a fair use, you can reply to that effect and see what action is taken next.

If you are actually sued for infringement, the copyright owner will need to prove the elements outlined in the beginning of this lesson. You then need to offer a defense such as fair use or some other limitation. If

FIGURE 15
Chilling Effects Clearinghouse

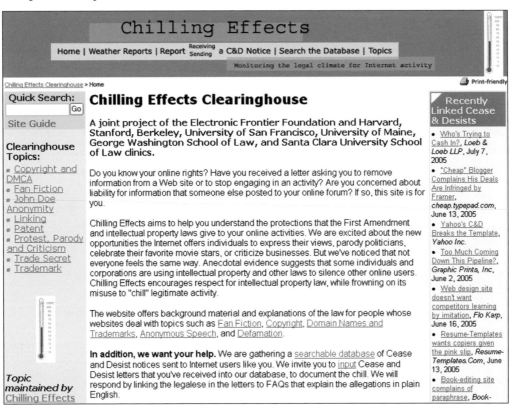

you are not successful and are found to have infringed, remedies for the copyright owner include:

- Injunction to stop your publication or distribution or performance or display of the infringing work
- Impounding and disposing of the infringing items
- Actual damages of the copyright owner such as lost profits or statutory damages of between $750 and $30,000, which may be increased to $150,000 for willful infringement or reduced to not less than $250 for innocent infringement; statutory damages are only available if the work was registered within the required time frame, as discussed in Chapter 1
- Court costs and attorney's fees (at the discretion of the court)

You also might be held criminally as well as civilly liable if you are a willful infringer. The criminal penalties are imprisonment, fines, or both. Prosecution for criminal copyright infringement is rare.

In addition to copyright infringement, you need to be concerned with possible trademark infringement for various materials you might be interested in using. Slogans, phrases, designs, images, characters, and symbols can all be trademarked. If you infringe a trademark, the possible penalties include:

- Injunction against use of the mark or use only under certain conditions
- Destruction of infringing articles

Monetary damages may include:
- The entirety of your profits
- The trademark owner's damages

- The costs of the lawsuit
- Possibly attorney's fees

If you find yourself in a legal action, the best first step is to seek competent legal advice. Relying instead on advice from your friends, something you heard about, or your bruised ego may seem a cheaper alternative, but most defendants can't afford to do without the guidance of an attorney who specializes in intellectual property law. Of course, the most economical course is to avoid the lawsuit in the first place—but as you have seen, this is not always possible.

UNDERSTAND THE
Public Domain

What You'll Learn

ARIZONA LOTTERY

▶ *In this lesson, you will learn about how some works move into the public domain or never fall under copyright.*

Public Domain Works

Works that are not copyright protected are in the **public domain**, available for everyone to use in any way they want without asking permission. Examples include:

- Ideas and facts
- Works that fall under the merger doctrine
- Works that are *scenes à faire*
- Laws from all levels of government, including court decisions and legislation
- Federal government documents such as agency reports and Congressional hearings
- A phrase, title, slogan, or name

QUICK**TIP**

Although a phrase, title, and so on is not eligible for copyright protection, it may receive trademark protection.

Works can also enter the public domain for other reasons, including:

- Expiration of the copyright protection
- The owner did not properly obtain copyright protection (because the owner didn't follow the directions)

The Merger Doctrine

Some works fall into the public domain because they are protected by what's commonly called the merger doctrine. As you have seen, ideas and facts are not protected by copyright and can be used by anyone without permission. The **merger doctrine** applies when there are a *very* limited number of ways to express an idea. If someone could copyright that expression, they would have a monopoly on the idea, which copyright does not allow. Therefore, where an idea and its expression are so intertwined, the expression can't be copyrighted. For example, rules for a contest or lottery usually sound the same because there are only a few ways to explain the legalities involved. Some cases involving software have discussed the merger doctrine because there are usually only a few *efficient* ways to write code that produces the desired result.

Figure 16 shows the FAQ pages for a few state lottery Web sites.

Scenes à faire are stock scenes, characters, and features of a work considered standard or essential to the genre or field. For example, setting a murder mystery in a large mansion on a dark and rainy night, starting a crime story with a mysterious woman walking into a private investigator's shabby office, or computer programs that use similar icons for performing functions such as opening, saving, and deleting files, are all examples of *scenes à faire*. A variety of cases involving software, music, and literary

FIGURE 16
State lottery FAQs

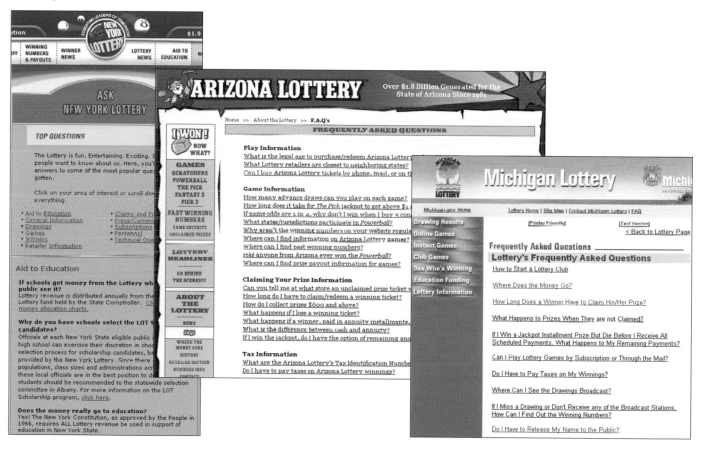

works have considered *scenes à faire* when determining infringement.

Acuff-Rose Music, a sheet music publishing company, sued Jostens (the class ring company) for copyright infringement for Jostens' use of the sentence, "If you don't stand for something, you'll fall for anything," in their ads. Acuff-Rose claimed this use was an infringement of the song, "You've Got to Stand for Something," the lyrics of which included "You've got to stand for something or you'll fall for anything." The court found that Jostens did copy the lyrics but that the lyrics were not original and had been in existence in the public domain before Acuff-Rose's property was created. Therefore, the phrase is not copyrightable and is not protected.

Abandonment of Copyright by Donation

Some people relinquish their copyright protection and dedicate their work to the public domain for everyone to use. Most often, though, they grant blanket permissions only for limited purposes, while other uses still require permission.

Chapter 4 discusses licensing and permissions in greater detail.

Moving In and Out of Public Domain

Some works have had their copyright restored as a result of international agreements such as GATT TRIPS. Artists who used what had been a public domain work had one year to remove it from their work, or else they could be sued for copyright infringement.

CONCEPTS REVIEW

Match each term with the statement that best describes it.

_____ 1. Derivative work

_____ 2. Tangible medium of expression

_____ 3. Digital watermark

_____ 4. Patent law

_____ 5. Trademark law

_____ 6. Intellectual property

_____ 7. Parody

_____ 8. Public domain work

a. Protections for inventions

b. A work that no longer has copyright protection

c. A recast work based on the original that is changed in some way

d. A perceptible means of experiencing a work

e. A creation from a human mind

f. Code embedded in a media file or transmission that can identify it

g. A satirical or humorous rendition of a copyrighted work

h. Protections for marks or symbols

Select the best answer from the list of choices.

9. Which of the following would not be considered when deciding if a use is fair use?

a. Whether the work is in the public domain

b. Whether the work is for nonprofit use

c. How widely the work is distributed

d. Whether there is a large market for the work

10. Which of the following situations best describes contributory infringement?

a. You host a Web site that provides links to businesses that check for plagiarism

b. You host a Web site for a local food bank with a photo you took of a garden

c. You host an innocuous-looking Web site that features a hidden link to copies of popular software and serial numbers

d. You host an innocuous-looking Web site that has thumbnail photos and links to their sites of origin

11. Which term best describes the merger doctrine?

a. Combining two copyrighted works into one

b. A transformative work

c. You can't describe the work any other way

d. You are only using a small amount of the original in your work

12. Which of the following is not a way a work can enter the public domain?

a. The author donates it

b. It is posted on the Internet

c. The author didn't fill out the copyright form correctly

d. The copyright has expired

13. Which of the following is most likely to be considered infringement?

a. You use images from an unreleased movie you downloaded to make a collage

b. You write a comedy sketch about a movie star's private life.

c. You use minimal material from an original work and send it to family

d. You create a Web site where users can download a licensed movie after paying a fee

Understand infringement.

1. Using your favorite word-processing program, start a document and save it as **Infringement_FairUse** in the drive and folder where you are storing files for this book.
2. Explain how a *de minimus* argument can affect a copyright suit being dismissed.
3. Explain why ASCAP could make the Girl Scouts pay for singing songs at camp. Extrapolate and make an argument whether people singing a song in the shower or in their car is infringement.
4. Explain why Bette Midler's case was a violation of her right to publicity but Tiger Woods' case was not.
5. Save your work.

Understand fair use.

1. List the four factors that make up the Fair Use doctrine.
2. Explain the differences between the Rogers/Koons (puppies) case and the Tom Forsythe/Mattel (Barbies) case. Why was one case infringement and the other not?
3. Explain how a nonprofit educational use can infringe copyright while a commercial use can be fair use.
4. Explain the difference between a derivative and transformative work.
5. Save your work.

Understand infringement legalities.

1. Explain how not establishing one of the elements that a copyright owner must prove might affect their case.
2. Discuss two elements a copyright holder must prove to win a suit against an alleged infringer.
3. Save your work .

Understand the public domain.

1. Describe three ways a work can enter the public domain.
2. Describe the merger doctrine.
3. Save your work, then close Infringement_FairUse.

One of your friends has developed two versions of a new online memory game, Neural Murals. In version I your friend created scenarios using celebrities in scenes from their movies. She found the photos online. In version II, your friend created fantastical or satiric situations by using image-editing software to mix scenes from two or more movies together. Your friend has already launched the games on the Internet, but was unprepared for the response from film studios. She's been told to expect cease-and-desist letters to arrive in a few days. Before she meets with her attorney, you thought you'd tap into the knowledge of copyright you've gained thus far and analyze each version with her to determine whether it is a fair use.

1. Open your favorite word processor, then start a new document and save it as **Neural Murals** in the drive and folder where you are storing files for this book.
2. For version I, what rights could they claim you violated or infringed?
3. For version II, apply each of the four factors of the fair use doctrine to the game, then state whether each factor would be considered fair use in this case.
4. Save the Neural Murals file, then close it.

You recently went to an exhibit of mixed media at a museum, where you took several photographs. Some pieces were new, others were copies of classics, and still others were busts of historical personages. Now, under fair use, you plan on using these ideas as a springboard for your own new projects. Before you begin, answer the following questions about your intended use.

1. Open your favorite word processor, then start a new document and save it as **Derivative Analysis**.
2. Using your intellectual property and fair use knowledge, answer the following:
   - Discuss the reasons for and against using the photos.
   - Can you make a clay model of a photograph of a Ferrari? What if you paint it in a different color?
   - The photo you took of a painting depicting Shakespeare's *A Midsummer's Night Dream* gave you the idea to create a new scene based on the play's plot and themes, using fruit and vegetables as the characters. Can you?
3. Save the Derivative Analysis document, then close it.

chapter

3

SEARCHING THE
Internet

1. Understand the Internet timeline.

2. Understand Internet search engines and tools.

3. Perform simple searches.

4. Perform advanced searches.

5. Search the invisible Web.

chapter 3 SEARCHING THE Internet

Most of us tend to use just one search engine, along with one simple search term, for all our searching needs. When we don't find exactly what we want, we assume it's because the information isn't out there and that our frustration is just part of the package. In reality, there are several tools we can use to improve our searches and many strategies we can use to find what we need. Understanding search engines—what they can do and how they differ—greatly increases your chances that what you search for is what you retrieve.

To understand search engines, we need to first step back and look at the development of the Internet itself. Figure 1 points out the highlights of this evolution, which are discussed in greater detail in Lesson 1. Most of us cannot begin to fathom the amount of

FIGURE 1
Internet timeline

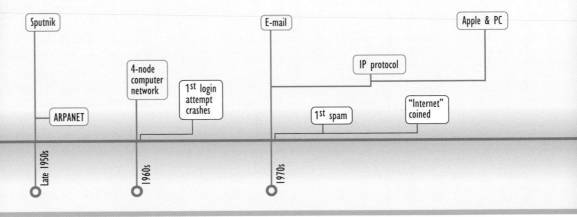

information on the Internet; its volume is of a magnitude of scale that is conceptually overwhelming, and its content changes from moment to moment. It has evolved from a small computer node to a complex global aggregate of computer networks involving millions of computers. Its popularity has enhanced and even altered the nature of communications exponentially—as did its technological ancestors, the telegraph, telephone, and radio. An overview of the development of the Internet will help to put its structure and resources in context so that we can work with it more successfully.

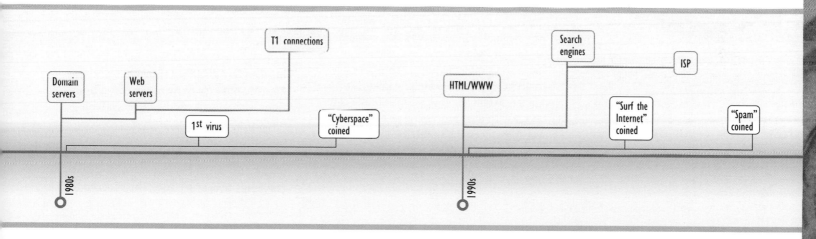

UNDERSTAND THE
Internet Timeline

What You'll Learn

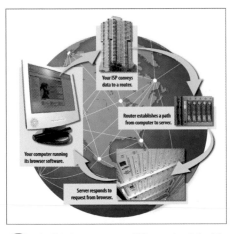

In this lesson, you will learn about the history of the Internet so that you better understand its structure.

Inspiration for the Internet

The impetus for creating what would become the Internet began as a reaction to the world's first artificial satellite, the grapefruit-sized Sputnik, launched in 1957 by the Soviet Union. See Figure 2. The U.S. government perceived the Soviet's technological achievement as a direct threat both to its national defense and to its scientific proficiency. As a result, the United States formed an agency within the Department of Defense to ensure the supremacy of U.S. military science and technology. At that time, the prevailing assumption held by the computer industry was that computers were best used as very large calculators, pure and simple. Figure 3 shows an early UNIVAC computer, weighing in at just under 30,000 lbs. It was a mainframe computer with dual processing power; each **central processing unit (CPU)** was 2.5 **megahertz (MHz)**, which isn't anywhere near the computing power of one of today's cell phones.

The newly created agency, the **Advanced Research Projects Agency (ARPA)**, promoted what was at the time a radical vision for computer technology: the theme of the computer as a communication medium first and foremost, with its arithmetic capabilities taking a second place.

QUICK**TIP**

Also in response to the perceived Soviet threat, and at the same time he created ARPA, President Eisenhower created the National System of Interstate and Defense Highways, which now extends over 43,000 miles.

In 1962, the U.S. Air Force, following an independent classified research track, was figuring out how to maintain communications with missiles and bombers after a nuclear attack. At the time, there were only 10,000 computers worldwide, most of which resided in the United States, but already the Air Force was also facing the challenge of data security; they needed to keep those communications secure from eavesdropping. Their research eventually led to the development of a protocol that would become the standard for transmitting data over the Internet. The **packet-switching protocol** is used to break a message into discrete packets before it is sent. A **protocol** is an agreed-upon format that determines how computers communicate their data to each other. Packet switching was attractive to the military because important information could be broken up, transmitted over different routes, even arrive out of order, and it would *still* be readable.

FIGURE 2
Sputnik satellite

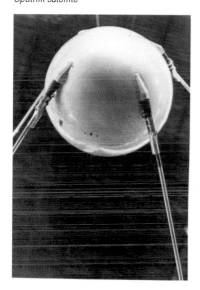

FIGURE 3
UNIVAC computer circa 1960

Each 8-inch tape held 1.4–5 MB of data

Toggle switches were used to program and input instructions

Console typewriter was output device

Early Internet Development

In late 1967, the Department of Defense funded an authoritative study on the "design and specification of a computer network." The display capabilities of monitors at the time were quite limited, as shown in the example in Figure 4. By 1969, very large computers linked the Stanford Research Center, the University of California Los Angeles (UCLA), the University of California Santa Barbara (UCSB), and the University of Utah. This 4-node network is considered the actual birth of the Internet—it transmitted data at the blistering speed of 50 **Kbps (kilobytes per second)**. The first international computer connection was made to the University College of London.

The early 1970s codified the achievement of people communicating over a distributed network, as well as a new combined communication protocol, later known as **Transmission Control Protocol/Internet Protocol (TCP/IP)**. TCP/IP handles the communication and exchange of data between different computers. In a paper describing TCP, its inventors Vinton Cerf and Bob Kahn coined the term Internet. Today there are dozens of Internet standards in use, ranging from Web pages to e-mail to blogs.

QUICK**TIP**

Downloading music from the Internet flourished in 1999 with the advent of Napster.

Emergence of the World Wide Web

The first iteration of the **World Wide Web (WWW)** was released in 1989 by the CERN group (the world's largest particle physics center, based in Switzerland) as an effective means for scientists to have access to automatic data sharing. They introduced **hypertext**, text that contains

FIGURE 4
Early computer monitor display

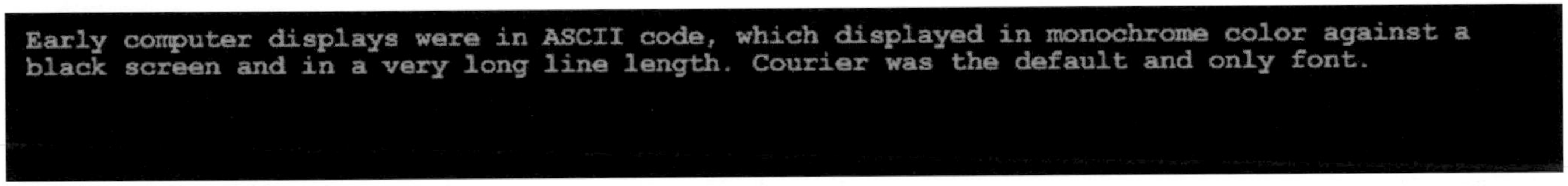

Early computer displays were in ASCII code, which displayed in monochrome color against a black screen and in a very long line length. Courier was the default and only font.

Comparing bandwidth

Bandwidth refers to the amount of data a digital connection can transmit in a set amount of time, usually measured in seconds. The bandwidth of the first commercially available dial-up modems was 14.4 Kbps, which would have taken over 40 minutes to download a large file of 4 MB (such as a typical song) off the Internet. In contrast, most high-speed connections today can download 4 MB in about 20 seconds.

links to additional information. Before long, the Web browser Mosaic incorporated **Hypertext Markup Language (HTML).** Figure 5 shows the graphic capabilities of an early Mosaic Web browser.

The HTML developed by Tim Berners-Lee at CERN established far-reaching technical standards. HTML became synonymous with the World Wide Web and has since been modified and extended into other computer languages. Perhaps equally distinctive was the ethical model Berners-Lee instituted with its release. He distributed WWW software for free and without royalties. He didn't even take out a patent on the software out of the passionate belief that Internet services should remain available and accessible to everyone, developer and end user alike.

QUICK**TIP**

HTML is the *lingua franca* that stipulates how a Web browser formats and displays text, graphics, sound, and other content. Among its definitive characteristics is the ability to turn text into hyperlinks, which are clicked to open additional documents.

The modernization of the Web began in earnest in the early 1990s with the proliferation of Web browsers designed with a graphical user interface (GUI), such as Mosaic. By the mid-1990s, **Internet service providers** (ISPs) provided public access to the Internet for personal, commercial, and other purposes. Current Web browsers such as Firefox, Internet Explorer, and Opera

FIGURE 5
Mosaic browser 1.0

Graphical interface

Hypertext links

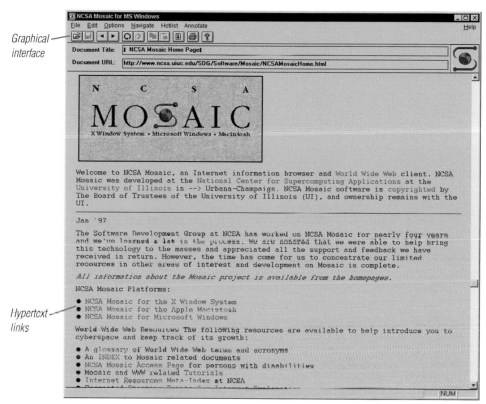

Famous first messages
The first telegraph message, sent in 1844, was "What hath God wrought?" suggested to Samuel Morse by Annie Ellworth, the young daughter of a friend. The first telephone call in 1876 from Alexander Bell told "Watson, come here. I need you." The first e-mail message sent by Ray Tomlinson in 1971 consisted of the top row of the keyboard, "QWERTYUIOP." In 1992, colleagues at British-owned Vodaphone wished each other a "Merry Christmas" text message.

locate and display pages containing graphics, sound, media, and interactivity that link the user to additional files and sites.

Evolution of Web Addresses

As the Internet and popularization of personal computers grew in the late 1970s and 1980s, the **Domain Name System (DNS)** helped make the interface more intuitive and clear. DNS servers translate **Internet Protocol (IP)** addresses (such as 204.127.195.15) into user-friendly domain names (such as *www.course.com*) and vice versa. An **IP address** is a unique string of four numbers separated by periods used to identify each computer or device that is online. Computers use IP addresses to establish connections and route traffic, but most people are more comfortable using the text-equivalent domain name.

A Web site address is known as a **Uniform Resource Locator (URL)**. The Web requires a protocol to transmit files over its network of sites, the most common of which is **Hypertext Transfer Protocol (HTTP)**. The initial information in a URL determines the protocol that a Web browser uses to retrieve a Web page. In addition to the protocol and domain name of the Web server, a URL can typically include a subdirectory and filename, such as *http://www.course.com/about/copyright.cfm*.

Breakthroughs for Public Web Users

For many years, the Internet was used exclusively for government, higher education, and research projects. At most universities, librarians were the power users, using the Web to put their collections online—second only to the computer science departments. The term *user friendly* was not in anyone's lexicon.

Throughout the 1980s, breakthroughs occurred such as the moderated newsgroups, known as **USENET**, which were the first community chat rooms. This initial practice of information sharing and discussion set an early and strong Netiquette precedent for free speech on the Internet. The Web community's advocacy of Internet free speech was demonstrated in 1996, when, in protest of passage of the overly restrictive Communications Decency Act, thousands of Webmasters kept their pages dark for 48 hours. The Supreme Court later ruled that the bill was unconstitutional, stating that the provisions intended to protect children from indecent speech were too broad and would infringe upon the free speech of adults.

Wireless communication

Whether wired with copper, cable, fiber optic, or wireless, any network capable of two-way communication can carry Internet traffic. **Wi-Fi (wireless fidelity)** uses a radio signal to connect computers. Although distances are increasing, most Wi-Fi connections are good up to 100 feet. Other wireless technologies include smart phones, a combination of cell phone and personal digital assistants (PDA) that can connect to the Internet over high-speed wireless networks. Bluetooth (named by Swedish company Ericsson after the tenth-century Scandinavian king) is an effective wireless industry specification for connecting and exchanging information between PCs, cell phones, printers, laptops, and digital cameras.

The Difference Between the Internet and the Web

The terms "Web" and "Internet" are often and mistakenly used interchangeably. While the Web is by far the Internet's most visible component, due mainly to its graphical user interface (GUI), it is in fact only one service of many. Conceptually, you can think of the Web as an enormous collection of files in various media stored on various computers, accessed through the Internet, viewed in a browser, and connected by hypertext links. Figure 6 shows how the Web works for a typical connection from your computer over the network.

Other Internet services include e-mail, instant messaging, online chat groups, and

FIGURE 6
How the Web works

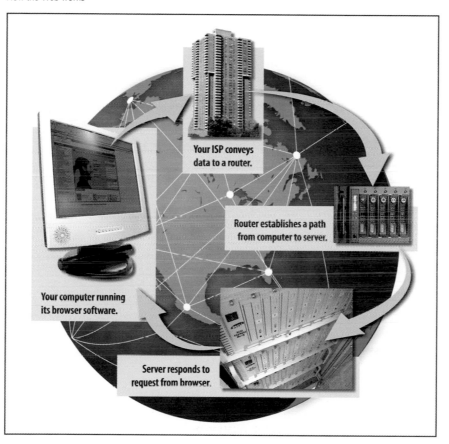

Your ISP conveys data to a router.

Router establishes a path from computer to server.

Your computer running its browser software.

Server responds to request from browser.

telephone calls, most of which have been integrated into the Web. For example, ftp (File Transfer Protocol) in the URL address indicates that files can moved between computers; http (Hypertext Transfer Protocol) transmits HTML files to a browser; and https (Hypertext Transfer Protocol over Secure Socket) allows the secure transfer of HTML files.

Internet Milestone Trivia

The following events provide an appreciation for how incidental occurrences became essential components of the modern Internet's construct and form.

- 1969: In the first attempt to use the Internet, the system crashed while the user was typing the *g* in *login*.
- 1972: Ray Tomlinson sent the first "real" e-mail message, which included the instructions for using the at (@) symbol. He came up with the now-standard @ symbol after spending about 30 seconds looking for an unusual key on the keyboard that could designate mailboxes on remote computers.
- 1978: Digital Electronics Corporation (a computer producer and developer of the early search engine AltaVista) sent the first unsolicited e-mail (aka spam, though this moniker had not yet surfaced) for a mainframe computer to all the ARPANET addresses on the West Coast.
- 1989-90: The first Web servers came online in Europe (the United States followed in 1991).
- 1990: Archie, the first Internet search engine, was developed. In deference to Linux file naming convention, the software name was shortened from *archive* to *Archie*. Subsequent search engines were named Veronica and Jughead, reportedly much to the disdain of Archie's developers.
- 1991: Web traffic comprised just 1 percent of all Internet traffic.
- 1992: Jean Armour Polly first published the term *surfing the Internet*.
- 1993: The term *spam* was associated with unsolicited e-mail messages. The association is derived from Monty Python's *Flying Circus*, an irreverent comedy sketch much adored by computer mavens.

Interestingly, Hormel Foods, the maker of SPAM, has never made an issue about its product's association with junk e-mail. They do, however, require that references to Internet-based spam be spelled in lower-case, so that their trademark, SPAM™, remains easily distinguishable.

QUICK**TIP**

Hormel's official definition of SPAM is *Specially Processed Assorted Meat.*

UNDERSTAND INTERNET SEARCH
Engines and Tools

What You'll Learn

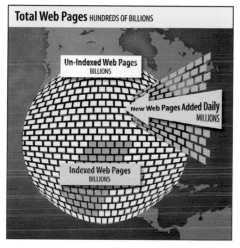

Total Web Pages HUNDREDS OF BILLIONS

Un-Indexed Web Pages
BILLIONS

New Web Pages Added Daily
MILLIONS

Indexed Web Pages
BILLIONS

 In this lesson, you will learn about Internet search engines, how they differ, and how they search the Internet.

The History of Searching the Internet

Back in the 1980s, finding a file on the Internet required you to know the name and location (including the precise com-puter, directory, and subdirectory) of the file you wanted. Expanded but not neces-sarily user-friendly searching began with Archie, a search program developed at McGill University in Montreal, Quebec. Figure 7 shows an Archie search for *IRC* (which stands for *Internet Relay Chat*, the first real-time multiple participant chat software).

The most successful pre-Web search engine was Gopher, developed at the University of Minnesota (and named allegedly in part for their sports mascot, the Golden Gopher). Among its many achievements, **Gopher** was used to access and search the first online collections at the Library of Congress.

With the advent of the Web, searching for information became a tangible—and marketable—commodity. A plethora of search engines have come, gone, and been bought out. Popular search engines that

Understanding FTP and HTTP

File Transfer Protocol (FTP) and Hypertext Transfer Protocol (HTTP) both transfer files, obviously, but with different purposes. FTP is used to physically upload or download files between your computer and a server, and usually requires a password for access. Seeing *ftp* in the URL instead of *http* indicates that you are connected to a file server instead of a Web server. In contrast, HTTP transfers files from a Web server to be viewed on your Web browser, but the files are not actually downloaded to your system, though you can save the contents of the viewed page using the Save As com-mand. Seeing *http* in the URL indicates that you are connected to a Web server.

have endured include AltaVista, America Online (AOL), Fast, Google, Lycos, Microsoft Network (MSN), Teoma, and Yahoo.

What Is a Search Engine?

A search engine is a software program designed to search and retrieve online data based on one or more keywords. A keyword is a significant word or phrase you type in the search text box of a search engine. There are three main types of Web search engines: indexes, directories, and pay per click.

How an Index Search Engine Works

An index search engine is a software program that sends software out to search the Web and retrieve pages that it then catalogs in a database, known as an index. When you perform a search, a mathematical formula matches and ranks your queries.

QUICKTIP

Google, which was founded in 1998, has the largest U.S. and global market share of all search engines.

FIGURE 7
Archie search

Find command

Keyword

Computer being searched

```
# `erase' character is `^?'.
# `search' (type string) has the value `sub'.

archie>  prog irc
# Search type: sub.
# Your queue position: 1
# Estimated time for completion: 5 seconds.
working...

Host ftp.cis.upenn.edu      (158.130.12.3)
Last updated 07:22 16 Nov 1994

    Location: /pub
        DIRECTORY      drwxrwxr-x      512 bytes   12:42   4 Nov 1994   ircs


Host ftp.tcp.com     (128.95.44.29)
Last updated 03:51 18 Nov 1994

    Location: /pub/QRD
        FILE      -r--r--r--      3529 bytes  13:08 20 Jun 1994   0QRD-BY-IRC

    Location: /pub/QRD/media/print
        FILE      -r--r--r--       269 bytes  03:11  6 Jun 1994   top.circulations.of.lgb.press

    Location: /pub/QRD/usa/federal
        FILE      -r--r--r--       384 bytes  18:00 26 Oct 1993   ninth.circuit.court.of.appeals
```

Search results

A search engine locates Web pages using a Web bot (short for robot), known as a spider or crawler. A **bot** refers to any computer program executed on the Internet that performs a repetitive or recursive function. A **spider** or **crawler** is a specific bot that methodically and routinely surveys the Web, following each hyperlink and logging the words it encounters in HTML fields or on the page to the index. Figure 8 shows the index search engine, Google.

When you type keywords in a search text box, the search engine applies a mathematical formula, known as a relevancy algorithm, to match the keywords to the content of the index. The search results are displayed as hyperlinks to Web pages ranked in order of relevance to your **search criteria**, all the words and qualifiers that make up your search statement. Note that when you query an index, the results you receive are only as current as the time the index was last refreshed. Because a search engine's index is always slightly out of date, your search results may occasionally produce an obsolete hyperlink, which appears as a **dead link** in your browser.

How Directories Work

A **directory** relies on human editors to physically populate the database by exploring sites, determining their logical placement in the directory, and then linking the sites to the directory. Hence, directories such as Yahoo preselect the body of available links, categories, and subcategories. Figure 9 shows the Yahoo directory search engine.

How Pay-Per-Click Searches Work

Over 90 percent of Internet users have used a search engine at one time or another. You

FIGURE 8
Index search engine

Google™

Web   Images   Groups   News   Froogle   Local^New!   **more »**

[Google Search   ] [I'm Feeling Lucky]

Advertising Programs · Business Solutions · About Google

Make Google Your Homepage!

©2005 Google - Searching 8,058,044,651 web pages

*Keywords search
indexed database*

FIGURE 9
Directory search engine

Keyword search available

Categories   Selected category

are no doubt familiar with the results that appear as a list of links, letting you click one that seems to fit your needs. What you may be less aware of is that many search engines partner with other Web sites to display links based on context keywords. **Pay per click (PPC)**, also known as **search advertising**, is when a company pays to have their site listed in the results when a user searches for certain keywords or phrases.

The goal of PPC is to entice the user to click the advertiser's link, often known as a **sponsored link**, before or instead of clicking the regular search results. Whenever a user clicks the paid link, the advertiser pays the search engine a fee. The fee is based on what the advertiser bid for the keywords. Most bids range from 5 to 99 cents per click, while highly coveted search terms can command much more.

PPC is a multibillion dollar industry. Many Web sites support PPC by allowing ads to appear in related Web pages. For example, you could navigate to a camping equipment Web site and find sponsored sites from travel agencies and outdoor magazines. Figure 10 shows samples of PPC advertising from two search engines.

Sometimes search engines (such as Yahoo) or large online retailers (such as amazon.com) gather personal data about you when you register on the site. That data can be combined with other data from their business partners to compile a profile about you. The information in the profile may or may not be correct, but there is probably little you can do about it because you don't even know it exists. Such profiles are used to tailor PPC advertising to your searches. To fully address privacy issues, it is a good idea to read the privacy pages of the search engines you use regularly.

The Open Directory Project

The Open Directory Project (ODP) is composed and maintained by a worldwide cadre of volunteer editors, who number in the tens of thousands. The directory is offered for free and focuses on "original, unique and valuable informational content that contributes something unique to the category's subject." Potential editors submit a form and are selected based on the numbers of editors already working on a topic, their Internet experience, interest in ODP, knowledge of their chosen subject, and affiliation with established Web sites. Other popular directories are based on contributions from, literally, anyone. Wikipedia is a "free content encyclopedia that is being written collaboratively by contributors from all around the world." Wiki (What I Know Is) refers to online collaboration software that allows users to create and edit content. Therefore, both amateurs and professionals can contribute to a topic. The veracity of newly added information is unknown, although egregious errors are usually corrected promptly. Many instructors do not permit students to cite Wikipedia as source because of the veracity issue. However, to ensure maximum neutrality, Wikipedia's policy dictates that articles should describe controversy, rather than actively advocate a position that embodies it.

Advertisers' conflict with search engines

The relationship between search engines and their advertisers is not without controversy. Search engines allow companies to buy keywords that are the proper names of competing businesses. The companies whose names are used allege that this is trademark infringement. In one case, GEICO unsuccessfully sued Google because searchers who included "geico" in their search criteria received sponsored ads from competing companies. In her ruling, the judge stated "As a matter of law it is not trademark infringement to use trademarks as keywords to trigger advertising." However, the judge also stated that while using Geico as a keyword was acceptable, a company using the word "Geico" in their sponsored ad text did dilute Geico's trademark and caused consumer confusion.

QUICK TIP

Other sources of data used to compile customer profiles include online surveys you fill out, such entering a contest or subscribing to a site.

How Search Engines Differ

The three most important qualities for a successful search engine are relevancy, relevancy, and relevancy. All search engines use the words they find in a Web page as

part of their ranking. However, each search engine uses its own proprietary algorithm for ranking and is constantly improving its

FIGURE 10

Viewing regular and PPC results

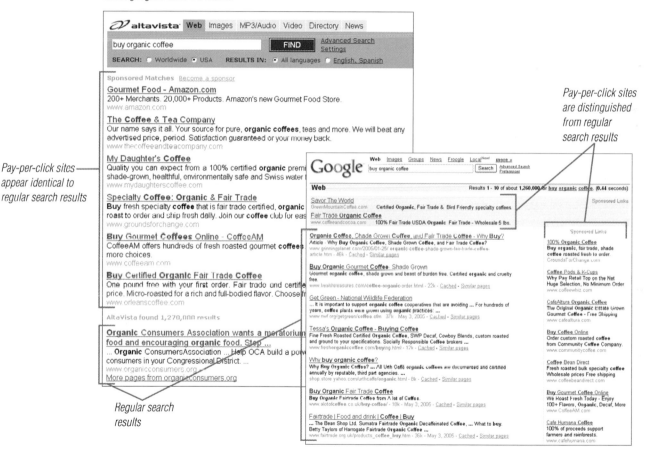

Pay-per-click sites appear identical to regular search results

Pay-per-click sites are distinguished from regular search results

Regular search results

algorithm. Search engines use some of the following text occurrences to rank pages:

- Words on the page: Words that appear higher on the page are weighted more than words than those that appear lower.
- Where the words appear: Keywords should always appear in the HTML title tag, and also in meta tags and in the headlines and first few paragraphs.
- Number of links to the Web page from other sites: The more sites that link to you, the better, but search engines can also determine if you set up dummy or artificial links and will penalize you.
- Each word in the first several lines of text: All keywords should appear prominently in whatever text your page lists first.
- A number of recurring words on the page: Keywords should repeat in a page, but if you attempt to stuff a page, the search engine will penalize or even exclude you.

As a searcher, you want the search engine to retrieve the links that are the most germane based on the keywords you typed. As a business, you want your site to be optimized so that spiders rank your page as high as possible when a searcher enters your keywords. **Search engine optimization (SEO)** is an industry devoted solely to helping Web sites improve their ranking (and visibility) in regular and PPC searches, particularly the latter. Another goal of SEO is ensuring that visitors take action instead of just browsing a site. The action may be as simple as filling out a form, but ideally it involves the transfer of money—yours. Figure 11 shows a sample SEO company.

SEO companies command a fee for their extensive services. However, you can easily register your Web site with several search

FIGURE 11
Sample SEO Web site

engines for free. Of course, the onus for determining the best keywords and phrases is on you.

Understanding Meta Tags

At the top, or **head**, of an HTML page is important information about the Web page. **Meta tags** contain words that a search engine employs in its indexing. Meta tags are a component of HTML; they are not visible on the Web page when it is displayed in your browser. You can view the source code for any Web page open in your browser by clicking View on the menu bar, and then clicking the menu command, such as Source (Internet Explorer) or Page Source (Mozilla Firefox). Figure 12 shows meta tag information for a Web page.

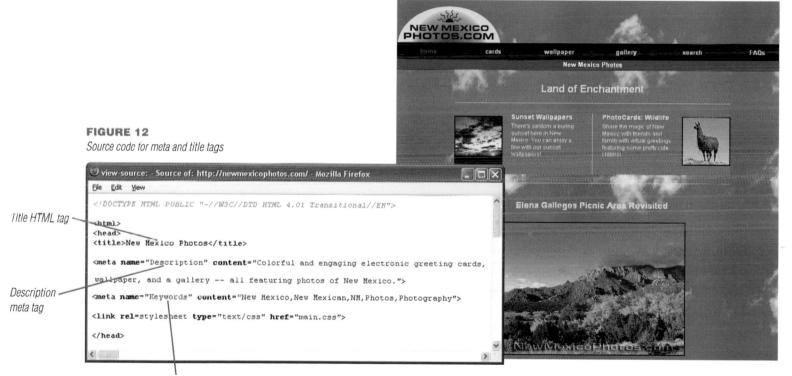

FIGURE 12
Source code for meta and title tags

Title HTML tag

Description meta tag

Keywords meta tag

Untangling the Relationship Between Search Engines

The relationship between the major search engine companies is a flow charting nightmare and often morphs into different intertwined associations. To appreciate their context, you must understand the following concepts:

- Who owns the search engine?
- What contracts exist between search engines?

- Who supplies the main/direct search results?
- Who supplies the pay-per-click search results?
- Who supplies the directory search results?

Overture supplies the bulk of PPC results to most major search engines except for Google, which powers its own. The DMOZ Open Directory Project (named after the Open Directory Project's domain name, Directory.Mozilla.org) supplies directory results to nearly all the search engines except for Yahoo, which powers its own. Answers to the other questions can become quite complex, as reflected in Figure 13. Note that the figure includes many, but not all, of the major search engines; for example, MSN powers its own main search and advertising.

FIGURE 13
Search engine relationships

YAHOO!		Google		overture
owns	**supplies results to**	**supplies results to**	**supplies PPC to**	**supplies PPC to**
alltheweb	alltheweb	AOL	AOL	alltheweb
AltaVista	AltaVista	Go	AskJeeves	AltaVista
Inktomi	Yahoo	Google	Go	HotBot
Overture	HotBot (via Inktomi)	iwon	Google	Lycos
yahoo		Netscape	iwon	MSN
			Netscape	Overture
				Yahoo

dmoz open directory project	TEOMA	
supplies directory to	**supplies results to**	**receives PPC from**
AltaVista	AskJeeves	AskJeeves (via Google)
AOL	InfoSpace	
Google	HotBot	
iwon	Teoma	
MSN		
Netscape		

Understanding Meta Search Engines

In addition to search engines that search their own index, **meta search engines** submit a query to a host of search engines, and then display the concomitant results. Dogpile, one of the most popular meta search engines, lets you choose whether to list the results by relevancy or group them by search engine. However, it intersperses in its results ads from pay-per-click advertisers. Others, such Vivisimo, list the results by relevance and also separately organize the results into categories and subcategories, so you search in a result cluster. **Clustering** groups results around a theme, which may include keywords or topics you would not have thought to include. Figure 14 shows search results for two meta search engines.

FIGURE 14

Meta search engines

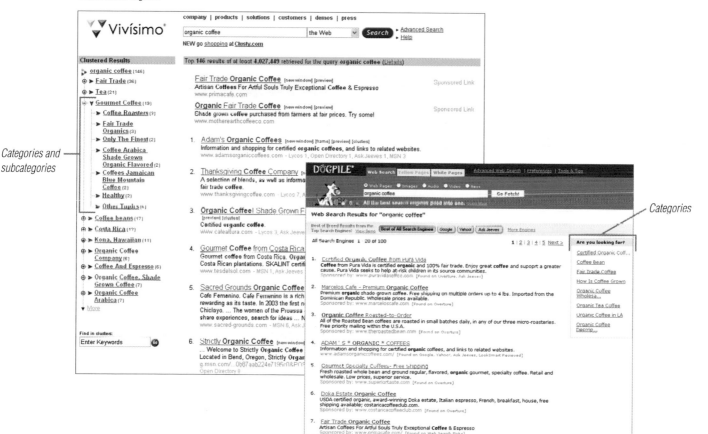

Categories and subcategories

Can You Ever Really Search the Web?

The Web contains hundreds of billions of documents residing on Web servers around the world. No single search engine is capable of locating, not to mention searching, anywhere near that amount. Regardless of the particular search engine or combination of search engines you employ, you will never be able to search more than a fraction of the total Web. Figure 15 illustrates the vastness of the Web.

FIGURE 15

Proportion of indexed to un-indexed Web pages

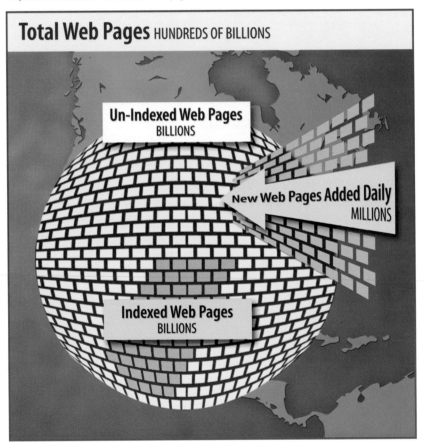

Total Web Pages HUNDREDS OF BILLIONS

Un-Indexed Web Pages BILLIONS

New Web Pages Added Daily MILLIONS

Indexed Web Pages BILLIONS

PERFORM
Simple Searches

What You'll Learn

In this lesson, you will perform simple searches and compare the results.

Using Keywords

Simply put, keywords allow you to retrieve information. Keywords are a useful starting point because you can easily add more or change their order in the search text box. Of course, it is always helpful to have some idea of what you are looking for.

QUICK**TIP**

The type of information you need determines the type of search you should use.

Many people are visual learners; that is, they think in pictures. It may be helpful to write down (in natural language sentences) what it is you are searching for. That way, you can easily identify the objects in your sentence, which are often your best keywords. You can also use a search strategizer to select search engines that best serve your needs.

An example of a search strategizer is shown in Figure 16. When you enter multiple keywords as the search criteria, search engines return results based on the occurrence of all the words. Even though a search engine searches on all the words in your criteria, it is always a good idea to vary the order of the search criteria so you can assess different results. Some algorithms weight the first word or words heavier than the subsequent ones. The most important point to grasp is that algorithms differ, which is why searching with identical keywords on different sites generates different results.

FIGURE 16

Search strategizer

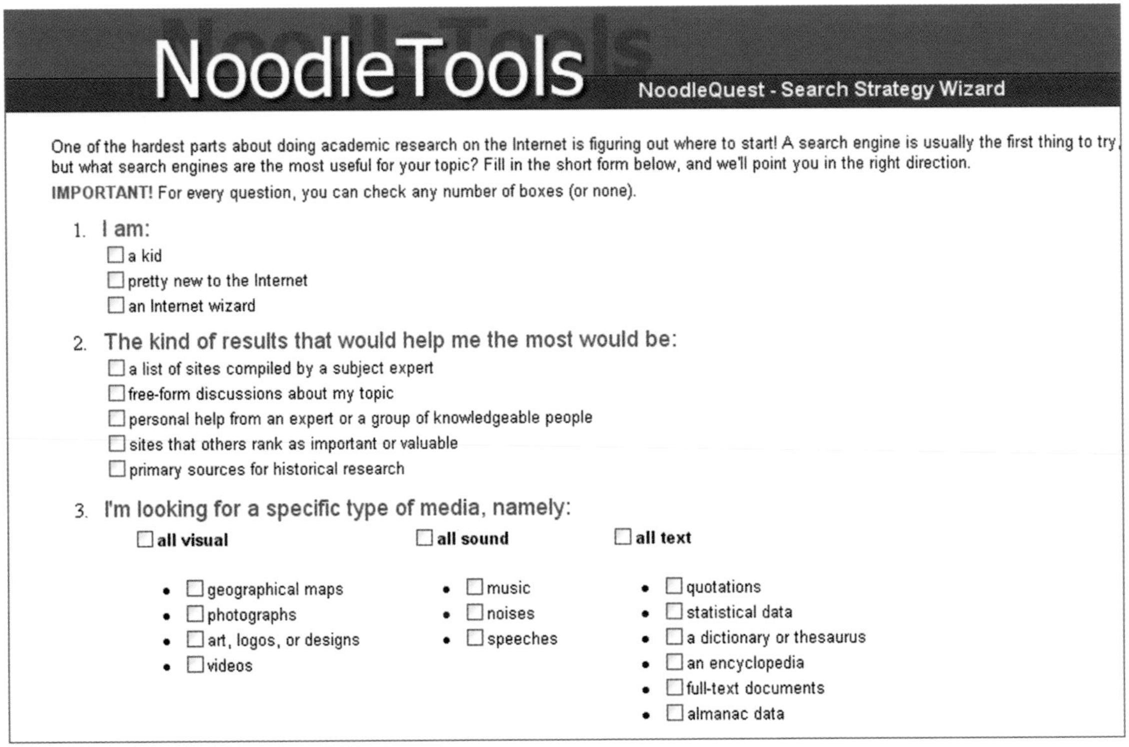

NoodleTools

NoodleQuest - Search Strategy Wizard

One of the hardest parts about doing academic research on the Internet is figuring out where to start! A search engine is usually the first thing to try, but what search engines are the most useful for your topic? Fill in the short form below, and we'll point you in the right direction.

IMPORTANT! For every question, you can check any number of boxes (or none).

1. I am:
   - ☐ a kid
   - ☐ pretty new to the Internet
   - ☐ an Internet wizard

2. The kind of results that would help me the most would be:
   - ☐ a list of sites compiled by a subject expert
   - ☐ free-form discussions about my topic
   - ☐ personal help from an expert or a group of knowledgeable people
   - ☐ sites that others rank as important or valuable
   - ☐ primary sources for historical research

3. I'm looking for a specific type of media, namely:
   - ☐ **all visual**
   - ☐ **all sound**
   - ☐ **all text**

   - ☐ geographical maps
   - ☐ photographs
   - ☐ art, logos, or designs
   - ☐ videos

   - ☐ music
   - ☐ noises
   - ☐ speeches

   - ☐ quotations
   - ☐ statistical data
   - ☐ a dictionary or thesaurus
   - ☐ an encyclopedia
   - ☐ full-text documents
   - ☐ almanac data

FIGURE 17

Google search results

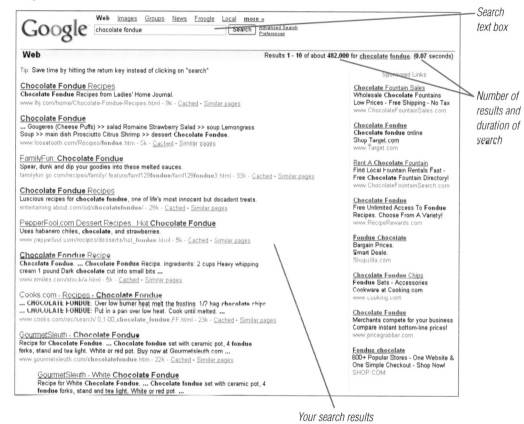

Search text box

Number of results and duration of search

Your search results will vary

Perform a keyword search

1. Connect to the Internet, navigate to the Online Companion, then click **Link 4**.

   The Google search page appears.

2. Click the **Search text box**, type **chocolate fondue**, then click **Google Search**.

   The search results, complete with PPC advertisers, appear in the new window, as shown in Figure 17. You can also view the number of results and the time it took to complete the search.

   TIP When you type keywords in lower-case, search engines return both upper- and lowercase matches.

3. Open a word-processing or graphics program, then save the file as **Keyword Search** in the drive and folder where you are saving files for this book.

4. Copy the search results and paste them into the new document.

   TIP You can also print the results by clicking File on the browser menu bar, clicking Print, then clicking OK in the Print dialog box. If you choose this alternative, skip Steps 3–5, and write *Keyword Search* at the top of the printout.

5. Save Keyword Search but do not close it.

You searched Google using keywords.

Add a keyword to search criteria

1. Type **fountain** in the Search text box following *fondue*, then press **[Enter]** (Win) or **[return]** (Mac).

   Additional results appear, as shown in Figure 18. For Google and other search engines, pressing [Enter] or [Return] obtains results faster than clicking the Search button.

   > **TIP** When adding several keywords, it is a good idea to list your most important keywords first.

2. Copy the results into the Keyword Search document, below the existing results, or use the Print dialog box in your browser to print the search results.

3. Compare the number of search results and time it took to complete the searches.

4. Note duplicate results from both searches, including the sponsored links.

   In a word processor, create an outline shape, such as a circle or square, over the duplicates. On paper, just circle the duplicates.

5. Save Keyword Search, then close it.

You added a word to the search criteria and then compared the search results.

FIGURE 18

Adding a word to the search criteria

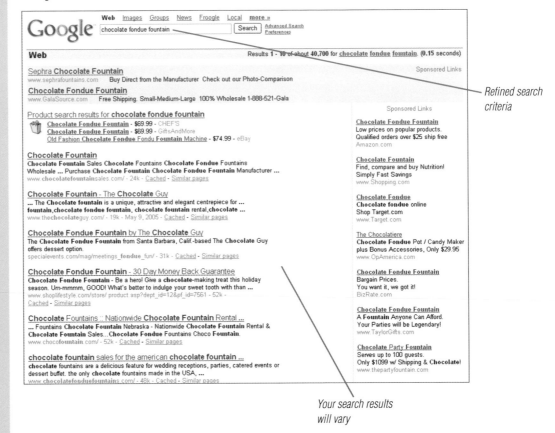

Refined search criteria

Your search results will vary

PERFORM
Advanced Searches

What You'll Learn

In this lesson, you will use advanced search features and Boolean operators to refine search criteria.

Using Advanced Search Features

Obtaining "good" search results is a function of sharply articulated search criteria; the better your query, the better your search results.

You can think of the contents of the Internet as one vast database. As with any database, you want your query to be specific enough so that you retrieve just the results you want. Fortunately, many search engines provide easy-to-use tools that make it simple to refine your search. For example, some search engines provide a link that searches just for specific information, such as images. Figure 19 shows the link for the image search tool in various search engines.

FIGURE 19

Image links for various search engines

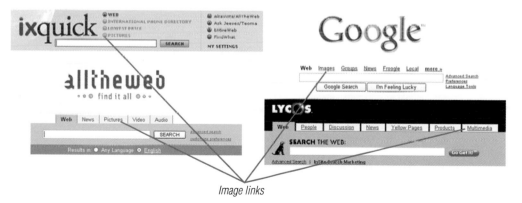

Image links

Boolean Operators

Many search engines also provide an advanced options page where, using a natural language interface, you can add, expand, or constrain your search criteria. With search criteria, you can easily specify what you want to retrieve by applying mathematical database functions to the algorithm. You can use **Boolean operators** to construct complex searches. A Boolean search uses operators that logically define the relationships between your search criteria. The most common operators are OR, AND, and NOT. By joining words and phrases with one or more operators, you can ensure that you receive relevant results while eliminating superfluous one. Common Boolean operators are described below:

- OR—Retrieves files containing at least one of the words or phrases
- AND—Retrieves only files containing all the words or phrases
- NOT—Excludes any files containing at least one of the words or phrases

Figure 20 shows how using these operators can alter the search results for barbeque sauce. The advanced search page varies between search engines and may even *vary within* the search engine depending on whether you are searching the Web, for images, news, and so on. You can use Boolean operators to construct very complex search statements, as shown below. For example, the search criteria *post war us OR europe "film noir" NOT "philip marlowe"* retrieves sites that reference film

noir movies produced after World War II in the United States or Europe that do not reference the name Philip Marlowe (a character who was a private investigator). Because the NOT operator excludes sites, you need to be careful when using it. In this example, any site that mentions Philip Marlowe would not appear in the search results.

QUICK**TIP**

The vast majority of searches use only one or two words. Only 3 percent of all searches use Boolean operators.

FIGURE 20
Boolean operator searches

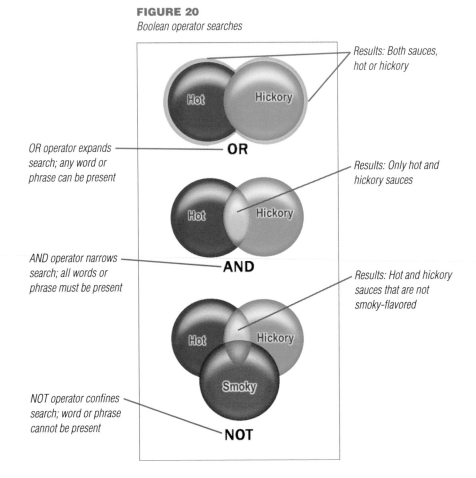

OR operator expands search; any word or phrase can be present

Results: Both sauces, hot or hickory

Results: Only hot and hickory sauces

AND operator narrows search; all words or phrase must be present

Results: Hot and hickory sauces that are not smoky-flavored

NOT operator confines search; word or phrase cannot be present

Table 1 lists Boolean operators and their equivalent symbols that you can use in the advanced search page of many search engines. If a search engine supports Boolean searches, you can type either name operators or symbols in the search text box. While typing words in text boxes on the advanced search page is effective, you can construct more complex searches by typing Boolean operators in the search engine's home page search text box. Note that some search engines also support abbreviations for wild card and truncated searches.

Many search engines also let you add text to search for a particular type of result or get a particular type of information. For example, typing *slide* at the end of your search criteria often retrieves slide presentations, such as PowerPoint, Breeze, or slide shows embedded in Web sites. Many search engines support searches for FedEx or UPS tracking numbers, patent numbers, UPC codes, telephone numbers, and so on. You can also retrieve specific information by typing a keyword, such as *define*: before a word to retrieve definitions of it from various glossaries and dictionaries, or *weather*

before the name of a city to retrieve links to weather in the area. For a list of specific search modifiers, check out the search Help systems of search engines and look for a link to tips, features, shortcuts, or similar words.

QUICKTIP

By default, when you enter multiple words in a search text box, most search engines search for all the words in the search statement and return results that contain one or more of them.

TABLE 1: Search Operators

operator	symbols	natural language	example
AND	+ or &	All of these words	papaya AND mango
OR	| or ,	Any of these words	dork OR geek
NOT	– or !	None of these words	coffee NOT decaf
exact phrase	" "	The exact phrase	"extraterrestrial lifeform"
parenthesis	( )	Groups criteria into sets	(alternative OR renewable) energy NOT geothermal
truncate	*	Searches for words that begin with with letters	horses, horseback, horsemanship
wildcard	?	Replaces letter(s) in the middle of a word	theater, theatre

Use an image search tool

1. Connect to the Internet, navigate to the Online Companion, then click **Link 5**.

   The Yahoo search page appears.

2. Type **neon light** in the Search text box, click **Images** above the Search text box, then press **[Enter]** or click **Yahoo! Search**.

   Images matching the keywords appear as thumbnails in the window, as shown in Figure 21. Search engines obtain image results based on filename, caption, surrounding text, and so on. The results may be from commercial or private sources, but both keywords must appear in the Web page.

   TIP Search engines that have multiple search categories, such as Web, images, news, or video, automatically apply the search statement to each category.

3. Open a word-processing or graphics program, then save the file as **Neon Search**.

4. Copy the search results and paste them into the Neon Search document, or use the Print dialog box in your browser to print the search results.

5. Save your work.

   You searched for images using keywords.

FIGURE 21

Searching images

Images search tool

Search total

Your search results will vary

FIGURE 22

Yahoo Advanced Image Search window (partial)

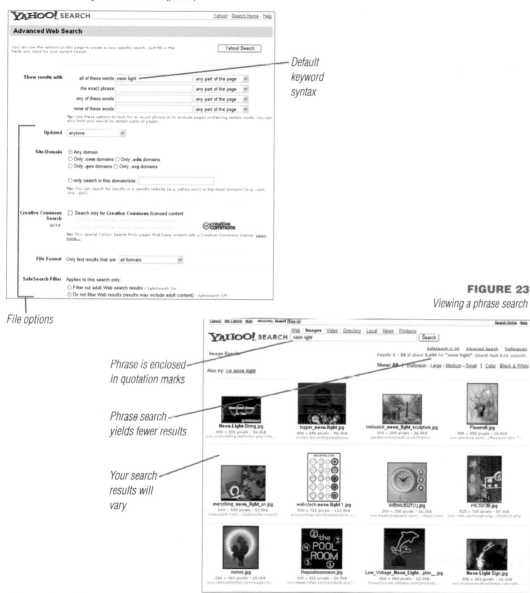

Default keyword syntax

File options

FIGURE 23

Viewing a phrase search

Phrase is enclosed in quotation marks

Phrase search yields fewer results

Your search results will vary

Use advanced search features

1. Switch to your browser if necessary, then click **Advanced Search** beneath the Search button on the Yahoo search page.

    The Advanced Search page appears, as shown in Figure 22, and displays the search terms you entered on the main search page. By default, the keywords appear in the all of these words text box, indicating that search results must include both keywords.

    > **TIP** Advanced search pages allow precision searches. In addition to the search syntax, search engines also provide additional search criteria, such as file type, date, site domain, and so on.

2. Cut **neon light** from the **all of these words text box** and paste it into the **exact phrase text box**, then press **[Enter]** (Win) or **[Return]** (Mac).

    Searching for an exact phrase narrows the search results and a different set of images appears, as shown in Figure 23.

    > **TIP** It is always a good idea to read the Help section for the default settings of search engines you have not used before.

3. Copy the results into the Neon Search document, at the end of the document, or use the Print dialog box in your browser to print the search results.

    > **| TIP** Scale the pasted images as desired.

4. Compare the number of search results in both searches, then note duplicates, if any.

5. Save your work.

You searched for a phrase and then compared search results.

Construct a complex search

1. Click **Advanced Search**, then type **art sculpture** in the any of these words text box, as shown in Figure 24.

   Your search results are confined to files that have the phrase neon light and either art or sculpture in the page.

   TIP It is not uncommon for multiple images from the same site to appear together.

2. Press **[Enter]** (Win) or **[return]** (Mac), then compare your screen to Figure 25.

3. Copy the results into the Neon Search document or use the Print dialog box in your browser to print the search results.

4. Compare all the search results, then note duplicates with the other searches, if any.

5. Save your work.

You added operators to the search criteria, and then compared search results.

FIGURE 24
OR operator added to search criteria

FIGURE 25
Viewing results of a complex search

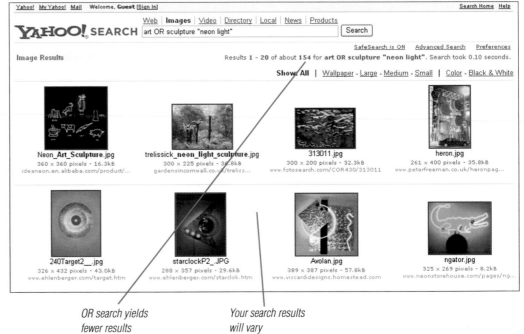

Either word is included in search results

OR search yields fewer results

Your search results will vary

SEARCH THE
Invisible Web

What You'll Learn

In this lesson, you will search for resources on the invisible Web.

About the Invisible Web

The term invisible Web conjures a technological underground, home to stealth expertise and cosmic conspiracies. But if you ask what is invisible to whom, the reality is less exotic. The invisible Web comprises mainly public sources of information that spiders do not index, which makes their content "invisible" to search engines. Figure 26 depicts the ratio of invisible Web pages to static searchable ones.

Much of the invisible Web is just that—invisible—because it is made up of dynamic databases that require a query from the

FIGURE 26
Relationship between invisible Web and searchable content

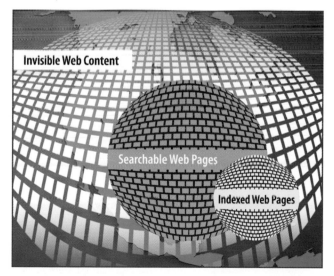

user in order to retrieve data. In a **dynamic database** or Web site, pages are not stored as individual files; instead, the content is created only when the information is requested. That is, dynamically generated pages do not exist until a user performs an action that produces the page, such as typing a query. Spiders do not query databases, so there is no source of information for them to search.

Spiders also bypass HTML pages embedded with a programming language known as a **script**, which adds functionality, such as up-to-date weather information, to a Web page. The goal of scripting is to create dynamic content of some kind, so again, there is nothing for spiders to search.

Estimates of the invisible Web suggest that invisible Web pages outnumber static pages by over 200 percent and outnumber the number of indexed pages by over 1000 percent.

Examples of dynamic databases include transportation, theater, weather information, maps, libraries, and laws.

Even static HTML content such as recently added Web pages are also invisible—until spiders can search them. Some estimate

that this delay may last up to a few months for new high-value Web pages.

Increasingly, more search engines are able to search non-HTML pages, such as Adobe Portable Document Format (PDF), Adobe PostScript, Microsoft Office, Corel WordPerfect, Lotus 1-2-3, and Shockwave Flash (SWF). Much of searching the invisible Web involves finding and querying dynamic databases, but there are also search engines designed specifically to search the invisible Web, such as a9.com, completeplanet.com, and invisible-web.net. An example of an a9.com search is shown in Figure 27.

FIGURE 27

Searching the invisible Web

Search results display in multiple categories

Select search results to display

FIGURE 28

Selecting a subject

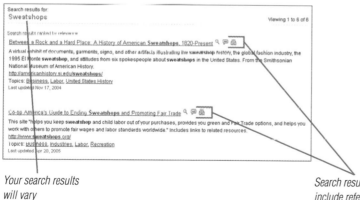

Enter keywords or click a subject

FIGURE 29

Viewing search results and subject references

Your search results will vary

Search results also include references to other searchable subjects

1. Connect to the Internet, navigate to the Online Companion, then click **Link 6**.

   The Librarians' Index to the Internet (LII) page appears, as shown in Figure 28. This search engine is designed to search the invisible Web and accesses thousands of annotated sites selected by librarians.

   > **TIP** Search engines with established listing criteria, such as LII, eliminate the need to investigate the veracity of information from unknown sources.

2. Click **Business**, notice the available subjects, click the **Search LII text box**, type **Sweatshops**, then click Search LII.

   Annotated search results appear, as shown in Figure 29. Each result also lists associated subjects.

3. Click a link of interest, review the content, and then return to the LII search results page.

4. Do not close your Web browser.

You used a search engine specifically designed to find invisible Web pages.

Search for databases

1. Click **Advanced Search**, type **clothing database** in the With all words (And) text box, then click **Search LII**.

   Links to various clothing-related databases appear, as shown in Figure 30.

2. Connect to the Internet, navigate to the Online Companion, then click **Link 7**.

   The Turbo10 page appears. Turbo10 allows you to customize the number of search engines it uses from its collection.

3. Type **forensic dna** in the search text box, then press **[Enter]** (Win) or **[return]** (Mac).

   The Topic Clusters tab lists the search results and number of results per topic, as shown in Figure 31. The Engines tab lists the search engines used and the number of results generated from each.

   > **TIP** Different browsers generate different topic clusters and results.

4. Type **database** following *dna* in the search text box, then press **[Enter]** (Win) or **[return]** (Mac).

   The search results display databases related to forensic DNA.

5. Click a topic in the Topic Clusters box, then click a database link of interest.

   Depending on the database link you select, you may be prompted to enter additional search criteria, to select a topic, and so on.

6. When you are finished, close your Web browser.

   You searched for and viewed databases related to a search topic.

FIGURE 30
LII database search

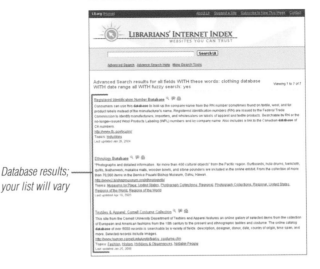

Database results; your list will vary

FIGURE 31
Turbo10 search

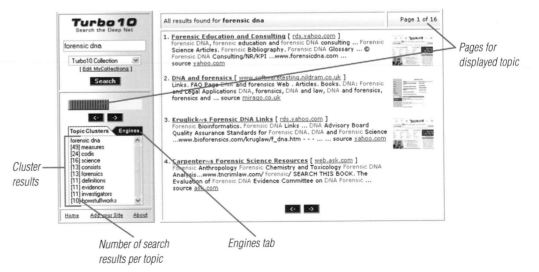

Cluster results

Number of search results per topic

Engines tab

Pages for displayed topic

Match each term with the statement that best describes it.

_____ 1. Boolean operator
_____ 2. Search engine optimization
_____ 3. HTML
_____ 4. Sponsored link
_____ 5. Invisible Web
_____ 6. Bandwidth
_____ 7. URL
_____ 8. Dynamic database

a. A text summary and hyperlink that a company pays to appear prominently in a Web page
b. Logical mathematical operators used to perform advanced searches
c. Content that is created on the fly in response to user input
d. The amount of data transmitted in one second through a connection
e. Improving keywords, text, and other aspects of a Web page to enhance the search results position
f. A language used in Web browsers
g. A Web site address
h. Public repositories of data not searched by search engines

Select the best answer from the list of choices.

9. Which of the following is *not* an example of search criteria?
   a. Phone NOT mobile
   b. "Fountain pen" antique
   c. Solar-powered race car kits that are only Formula 1 race cars
   d. "Digital camera" 7 MP OR 8 MP

10. What is a search strategizer used for?
    a. To optimize your Web site
    b. To automatically translate natural language to Boolean logic
    c. To help select the most appropriate search engine
    d. To write HTML

11. Which term best describes pay per click?
    a. Search advertising
    b. Search engine optimization
    c. Search criteria
    d. Clustering

12. What does a meta search engine do?
    a. Searches multiple search engines
    b. Produces only sponsored search results
    c. Searches the meta tags of Web pages
    d. Methodically searches the Web for new Web pages

13. Which of the following is not a function of a directory?
    a. Clustering
    b. Human-edited pages
    c. Sponsored results
    d. Content not searchable by search engines

14. Which is *not* an option typically offered on the advanced page of most search engines?
    a. Exclude pay per click
    b. File type
    c. Domain
    d. Date

15. Which type of search engine is associated with a relevancy algorithm?
    a. Virus checker
    b. Index
    c. Directory
    d. Invisible Web

Understand the Internet timeline.

1. Using your favorite word-processing program, answer the following questions. Save the document as **Internet Highlights** in the drive and folder where you are saving files for this book, include your name at the top of the document, and print a copy of it when you are finished.
   a. How did the U.S. government respond to the threat to its national defense and scientific expertise in the late 1950s?
   b. What are two advantages of the packet-switching protocol?
   c. What is the relationship of HTML to the World Wide Web?
   d. How did early browser displays differ from the ones we use today?
   e. What are the differences and similarities between an IP address and a domain name?
   f. What is the relationship between the Internet and the Web?

Understand Internet search engines and tools.

1. Using your favorite word-processing program, answer the following questions. Save the document as **Search Engine Highlights**, include your name at the top of the document, and print a copy of it when you are finished.
   a. Why can you never search the entire Web at one time?
   b. What role does a relevancy algorithm play in an index search engine?
   c. What are two differences between a directory search engine and an index search engine?
   d. How does pay-per-click advertising work?
   e. List three ways a spider can search a Web page.
   f. How does clustering differ from a directory?

Perform a simple keyword search.

1. Connect to the Internet, navigate to the Online Companion, then click **Link 8**.
2. Type **hybrid car** in the search text box, then search for the keywords.
3. Open your favorite word-processing or graphics program, then create a new document called **Keyword Search2** in the drive and folder where you are saving files for this book.

4. Copy the results into the Keyword Search2 document. (*Hint*: You can also print the search results.)
5. Save your work.

Add a keyword to the search criteria.

1. Type **review** in the search text box following car, then search for the keywords.
2. Copy the results into the Keyword Search2 document at the end.
3. Compare the results, then note the number of search results and overlapping results.
4. Save your work, then print and close Keyword Search2.

Use an image search tool.

1. Navigate to the Online Companion, then click **Link 9**.
2. Type **tent lightweight** in the search text box, then search for pictures.
3. Open your favorite word-processing or graphics program, then create a new document called **Tent Search** in the drive and folder where you are saving files for this book.
4. Copy the search results into the Tent Search document.
5. Save your work.

Use the advanced options tool.

1. Verify that **Link 9** is still open in your browser.
2. Open the Advanced Options page.
3. Type **tent lightweight** in the All the words text box, type **season** in the Must have text box.
4. Type **1 person** in the Must not have text box.
5. Type **backpack** in the Should have text box, then perform the search.
6. Search for Pictures with this search criteria.
7. Copy the results and paste them into the Tent Search document, then compare the results with the first set.
8. Note the number of search results and overlapping results.
9. Save your work, compare your screen to Figure 32, then print and close the document.

Search the invisible Web.

1. Navigate to the Online Companion, then click **Link 10**.
2. Type **appellate court** in the search text box, then search for the keywords. (*Hint*: Wait for the Discovering Results page to finish searching.)
3. Click a site of interest and review the content.
4. Type **slide** following *court* in the search text box, then perform the search.
5. Click a link of interest. (*Hint*: Some presentations may offer a View graphic version option, which you should click.)
6. Open your favorite word-processing or graphics program, copy the slide that appeared when you viewed the presentation and paste it into the new document, then navigate to the first slide in the presentation and copy and paste that one also.
7. Save the file as **Court Slide**, then compare your slides to Figure 33.

FIGURE 32
Completed Skills Review (1)

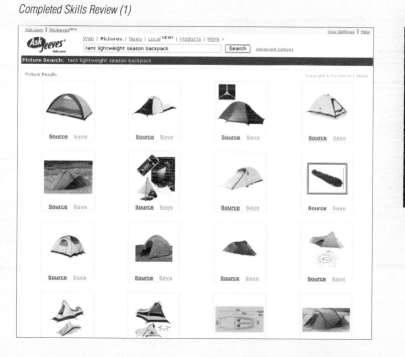

FIGURE 33
Completed Skills Review (2)

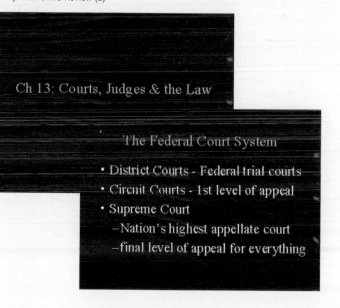

You are the new research assistant to the vice president in charge of new product development at Bocado Bites, a snack company. Your boss has an annoying habit of telling you to search the Internet on a general topic, only to then demand specific results at your meetings. You've learned to ask questions to figure out what he really wants. You translate his ramblings into advanced search criteria (incorporating Boolean operators) and then perform the search in two search engines.

1. Connect to the Internet, navigate to the Online Companion, then click **Link 4**.
2. Enter criteria in the Advanced Search page of the search engine to find information on the latest topic of interest from your boss: seaweed or nori rice crackers that have tamari flavoring but no wasabi. (*Hint*: Type Boolean operators in uppercase.)
3. Open your favorite word processor, copy the Find Results criteria from the Advanced Search page and paste them into the document, then save the file as **Rice Cracker** in the drive and folder where you are saving files for this book.
4. Perform the search, copy the search results into the Rice Cracker document, then save your work.
5. Click **Link 11** in the Online Companion.
6. Open the Power Search page, then using your experience in Step 2 as a guide, type the search criteria in the Power Search fields.
7. Copy the search criteria into the Rice Cracker document.
8. Perform the search, then copy the search results into the Rice Cracker document.
9. Compare the search criteria as interpreted by each search engine. Note the differences, number and type of search results, and so on. (*Hint*: View the entire line of search criteria at the bottom of the page.)
10. Save the Rice Cracker document, then close it.

The art museum you work for is under severe budget restraints, but needs to redo its Web page and institute its own search engine optimization plan. Although very few people volunteered to take on extra work double-checking Excel spreadsheets, several coworkers have tossed in their hats to work on the Web page. Therefore, the IT supervisor has devised a test to determine who gets the job: each person will assign keywords for random Web sites, which will then be evaluated for their effectiveness. You will be presenting first at the next staff meeting, so you get to work right away.

1. Open your favorite word-processing or graphics program, then create a new document called **Uncompensated Work** in the drive and folder where you are saving files for this book.
2. Navigate to the search engine of your choice, then perform a phrase search on *site of the day*. (*Hint*: Try to pick an index search engine, such as Google or Ask Jeeves.)
3. Visit a page selected as site of the day, then copy the screen into the Uncompensated Work document.
4. Return to the search results, navigate to the tenth page of the search results, visit a few sites on the tenth page, then copy the screen of a site of interest into the Uncompensated Work document.
5. Repeat Step 4 for the twentieth page of the search results.
6. Close any open Web pages.
7. Examine each Web page in the Uncompensated Work document and in your browser, then address the following topics:
   - At the bottom of the document, list the keywords and phrases you feel would be most appropriate for the art museum. (*Hint*: If you don't fully understand the site's topic, feel free to search the Internet to learn more about it.)
   - Review the page, then type what you know about how current the page is. (*Hint*: List the date the site was last updated or any identifying dates on the site.)

   - Compare how the more deeply linked search results differ from the first page of search results and each other.
   - Were the results what you expected? What was different?
8. Perform a search for a site using the keywords and phrases you selected, then evaluate the results.
9. Save the Uncompensated Work document, compare your pages to Figure 34, then close the document.

FIGURE 34
Sample Completed Project Builder 2

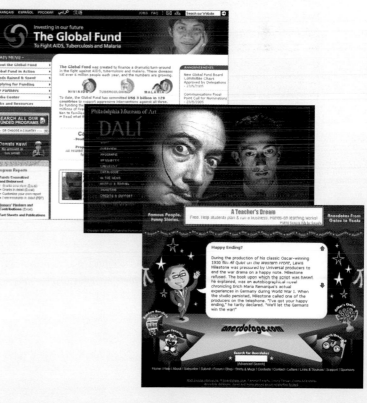

chapter 4

FINDING AND ACQUIRING
Images and Media

1. Understand licenses and permissions.

2. Understand media files.

3. Find clip art and Web art.

4. Find photographs.

5. Find video.

6. Find audio.

7. Find media at the Library of Congress.

chapter 4 FINDING AND ACQUIRING
Images and Media

The knowledge you have gained in intellectual property rights and copyright helps put in context the unique challenges the Internet brings to this type of law.

Applying finely honed Internet search skills makes your searches more accurate and expedient. Add some simple techniques for finding a copyright owner's intent for others using his or her material, and the combined skill set gives you the power to locate nearly any media on the Internet and then use it appropriately.

When you find a file you want to use, you should always presume that the file is protected by copyright. From that safe (if potentially daunting) first assumption, you can follow a simple method for ascertaining exactly what, if any, limits to using the material exist. The diagram in Figure 1 offers a simple series of steps to help you determine whether you can use a file.

Thousands of copyright holders of various media are committed to sharing their content outright. Many others may simply expect that you ask permission—which is exactly within their legal rights. Still others,

often businesses, require that you pay a fee or subscribe to a service in order to use the material in your own work. Regardless of the situation, you can enrich your professional and personal projects with wonderful online content while minimizing the risk of a legal action being brought against you if you practice due diligence in searching for content and gathering permissions.

Finding Sites

We know that the Web is home to tens of thousands of images and other media waiting to be downloaded, and several ambitious people have compiled links to sites for just this purpose. The lists are of various lengths, and because they are not always regularly updated, their currency—and value—varies. There has been heretofore no large-scale coordinated effort to compile a list of sites with usable media. *The Surf and Turf Index of Online Resources* is an effort to index and annotate these sites on a larger scale. It is by no means complete, but it does provide a starting point.

When performing your own searches for media, the easiest places to look are: stock photography, sound, and video sites; U.S. and state government agencies; the Library of Congress; universities; libraries; and organizational, personal, and commercial photo-sharing sites. Libraries in particular can be a great resource. Aside from having a wealth of material available online, their catalogs may also contain usable media not yet digitized or posted on their Web site.

Some Web sites and blogs specifically focus on links to usable material. Other sites to consider are sites that have digitized their image collections: newspapers, magazines, museums, and galleries.

FIGURE 1
Determining use diagram

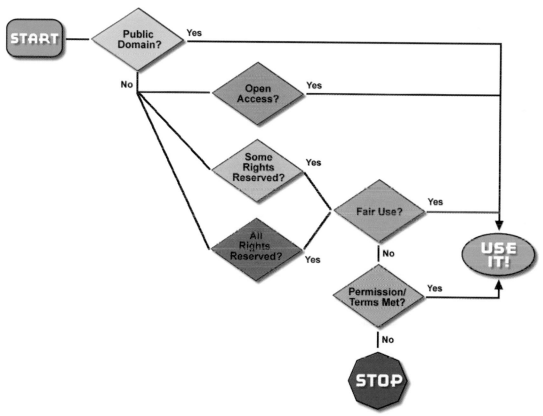

Stock images and media are available for a fee. Their advantage is that the work is high quality and professional. You can download files from the site or receive a CD of commercial-quality files; some even offer a few free files you can sample. Other sites offer a subscription service to a variety of clip art, illustrations, photos, sound clips, and so on. Figure 2 shows the media available at the clipart.com subscription site. Most fee-based sites let you try out low-resolution versions of an image for positioning in your document before deciding what you want to purchase.

QUICKTIP

Some subscription services post work by non-professionals. Although this content may not always be up to the highest professional standards, it's usually of acceptable quality and may be suitable, depending on the project.

FIGURE 2

Media available at a subscription site

Available media

Understanding open content and open source

Many organizations are committed to copying or sharing online matter in all file formats. By definition, open content is in the public domain, is a form of **copyleft**, meaning that it has generous sharing and derivative rights designation. The open source movement was begun by GNU (Gnu's Not Unix, a recursive acronym). It is a method for making a software program or other work free and requiring all derivative works be free as well. Its central argument is that software applications improve faster when the source code is available to programmers. Opposing views, embodied by Microsoft and others, maintains that open source removes the financial incentive to innovate and create new software.

UNDERSTAND LICENSES
and Permissions

Creative Commons is a nonprofit that offers a flex›

Audio
music, sounds,
speeches...

Images
photos, illustrations,
designs...

Video
movies, animations,
footage...

Find
Music, photos, and more

In this lesson, you will learn about terms of use, how to locate a file's term of use, how to obtain permission for use, and different copyright models.

Determining Use

Whether you use material appropriately is a function of your ethical values and your comfort in taking risks; many people base their actions on what they think their chance is of getting caught. The diagram for determining use in the beginning of this chapter is useful as general guide for negotiating the various paths from terms of use to your use.

Understanding Licensing Agreements

To decide whether to use a work of intellectual property, such as an image or a sound file, you find on a Web site, you must decide whether you can comply with its licensing agreement. A **licensing agreement** is the permission given by a copyright holder that conveys the right to use the copyright holder's work. There are many types of licensing agreements: royalty-free or rights-managed agreements, and exclusive or non-exclusive.

When someone other than the copyright holder wants to use the owner's intellectual property, whether for a high school play, broadcasting on the Internet, or including it in a fast food ad, they usually pay a royalty for that right. A **royalty** is the fee paid to a copyright owner, such as an artist, author, or musician, for the right to use their work. While the vast majority of artists make little off of royalties, consider Bobby Pickett, who wrote and performed the novelty classic Halloween song, "Monster Mash," or the heirs of Mel Tormé, writer of the "The Christmas Song" (Chestnuts roasting on an open fire...). They receive a royalty payment each time the song is played. Some authors or song writers receive an advance against their royalty payments, usually a percentage, based on how successful the publisher thinks the product will be. Some royalty payments are nonreturnable—if the book does not sell as expected, the author does not have to return the advance.

A **royalty-free agreement** means that a user can buy the right (license) to use a work on multiple occasions and for an unlimited amount of time. The art is available to any number of purchasers, making it a **non-exclusive license**.

Images can also be **rights-managed**. Under this usage, you can purchase images and have the exclusive rights to use them based on geographic location and under a certain time frame. An **exclusive** license is granted to a single user, and its use is restricted to specific conditions. The amount you pay is based on your intended use, considering such elements as size (billboard versus Web banner ad), distribution (Web page versus magazine print ad), and so on. The fee for exclusive licenses is usually considerably higher than for non-exclusive use because it lets the purchaser use the work in a given market without fear that a competitor will use the same piece (in a competing ad, for example). Figure 3 shows the home page of Comstock Images, a large commercial stock photography site that offers royalty-free images.

Another common but potentially confusing term is **copyright-free**. The technical definition is that *copyright-free* is the same as *royalty-free*. Americans tend to misuse the term to mean works that are in the public domain. It is obviously very important that you clarify its meaning with the owner before you use the material.

FIGURE 3
Stock photography site

Understanding Terms of Use

The rules that a copyright owner uses to establish use of their work are known as **terms of use**. For example, an artist grants permission for someone to use the work (license) under certain conditions (terms of use). However, on many Web sites, an author may state that the license is identical to the terms of use. Ideally, the terms should clearly identify what can and cannot be done to the work. Figure 4 shows sample terms of use.

When looking for copyright information on a Web site, you'll soon learn that there is no universal standard on where terms of use appear or how informative they are. Some copyright holders may define their terms explicitly; others may use terms incorrectly or make broad assumptions, such as what constitutes personal use.

The assumption of both copyright protection and a user's agreement to the site's terms of use are implicit in anyone's use of a Web site.

However, even when terms of use are clearly stated on a site, some users interpret them very loosely, or not at all. For example, many people genuinely believe that any file on the Internet on which you can right-click and save to disk is in the public domain—after all, it wouldn't be so easy to download if it weren't, right? Conversely, some Web sites erroneously assert copyright protection over public domain materials simply because they have placed them in their collection.

FIGURE 4

Sample terms of use

Sound Files and Sound Effects:

Note: Some of the free sound files on these web sites may be copyrighted and cannot be used without permission. Please check the copyright notice on each individual web site, and obtain permission from the copyright holder, if necessary.

What rights come with my footage?
All footage is copyright cleared, either because it is in the Public Domain or because the copyright owners whose libraries we represent have licensed it to us. Music, trademarks, logos, talent, and other underlying rights are subject to additional fees which must be negotiated on a case-by-case basis. (Also see: Client agreement).

Frequently Asked Questions

Restrictions on use of our Images

You can do anything you want with our images, EXCEPT CLAIM AUTHORSHIP AND/OR SELL THEM. Display them on your personal or commercial website; print them on banners or use them in Kiosk and Flash presentations; distort them in Auto-Illustrator or motion-fade them in Photoshop...it's up to you.
The detailed License Agreement and Terms of Use applies to all our material.

Even when you have the best intentions, you may find that your interpretation of a work's terms of use doesn't always match that of your host's. That is often because the terms may include common words such as *personal*, *educational*, *commercial*, *internal/corporate*, *nonprofit*, and *free/public* domain, and those words mean different things to different people. Most people assume personal use refers to one's private, not professional life. But the copyright owner might not have considered you using their work in a personal Web page (theoretically published for all to see), business or greeting card, or as your avatar in a chat room. Perhaps their definition of educational use is K-12 only, or the instructor can use material but students cannot.

Similarly, few people understand the legal status of a nonprofit organization when they say "for nonprofit use only." A nonprofit organization can range from a local cancer support group to a hospital with a staff of 7000 to an international disaster relief organization.

Locating Terms of Use

Nearly every Web site explains how others may or may not use its content, but where they keep this information varies from site to site. Look for links to Terms, Terms of Use, Copyright, FAQ, About Me, About Us, Use, Usage, Contact Us, and so on.

Sometimes you may need to open the photos or image page before reaching the copyright links. Some sites make it easy and post their terms of use prominently on the home page.

Other sites may state a specific use and then go on to explain that the material cannot be used, altered, copied, distributed, linked to, or transmitted without written permission. Note that many copyright holders who allow use of their material may also request that you notify them how you will be using the file, or they may, at the very least, request that you credit their work in some manner.

Obtaining Permission or a License

The permissions process is specific to what you want to use (text, photographs, music, trademarks, merchandise, and so on) and how you want to use it (school term paper, personal Web site, book illustration, fabric pattern). And, getting permission from an amateur photographer whose work you found on a photo-sharing Web site is different than getting permission from a large corporation. How you want to use the work determines the level and scope of permissions you need to secure. The fundamentals, however, are the same. Your request should contain the following:

- Your full name, address, and complete contact information
- A specific description of your intended use; sometimes including a sketch, storyboard, or link to a Web site is helpful
- A signature line for the copyright holder
- A target date when you would like the copyright holder to respond; this can be important if you're working under deadline

Figure 5 shows a sample request letter.

Locating Whom to Ask

Depending on the work, the creator may not always be the copyright holder; they may have sold or granted their copyright to a publisher, a record company, film studio, or another person or company. It is important that you locate the true copyright owner. For example, documentary filmmaker Jon Else shot a 4.5-second scene of San Francisco Opera stagehands in a backstage room watching television (which happened to be showing an episode of *The Simpsons*) during an opera performance. He had permission to use everything except the few seconds of the *Simpsons* episode. He obtained permission from *Simpsons* creator Matt Groening and the show's production company, Gracie Films. However, the Fox Broadcasting Company, Gracie's parent company, refused to grant permission and charged Else $10,000 for the few seconds of inadvertent screen time. Mr. Else elected to delete the *Simpsons* material and edit in other work instead.

The issue of getting permission becomes even more complicated when you consider using music or multimedia. For a song, you may need to locate the lyricist, the composer, and the owner of the sound recording. Multimedia presents an even bigger challenge. By definition, multimedia can contain video, animation, text, still photos or graphics, and sound. You have to

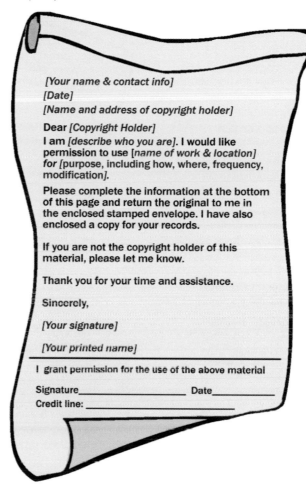

FIGURE 5
Sample request letter

[Your name & contact info]
[Date]
[Name and address of copyright holder]

Dear [Copyright Holder]
I am [describe who you are]. I would like permission to use [name of work & location] for [purpose, including how, where, frequency, modification].

Please complete the information at the bottom of this page and return the original to me in the enclosed stamped envelope. I have also enclosed a copy for your records.

If you are not the copyright holder of this material, please let me know.

Thank you for your time and assistance.

Sincerely,

[Your signature]

[Your printed name]

I grant permission for the use of the above material

Signature_____ Date_____
Credit line: _____

obtain permission from each copyright holder in each medium.

Remember that if you use copyrighted material without permission, you are setting yourself up for unhappy legal action. Once discovered, you will probably first be issued a cease-and-desist letter. Such a letter states when and how you copied the work without permission, demands that you immediately stop the use and distribution, and demands that you respond that you have performed this action by a certain date. Otherwise, further legal action can and will be taken against you. For example, in early 2004, musician Brian Burton (aka DJ Danger Mouse) mixed music from Jay-z's the *Black Album* and the Beatles' *White Album* to make the *Grey Album*. His original intent was to only make a few thousand copies, not to distribute it widely. However, the album was immediately picked up by other Web sites and soon caught the attention of Capitol Records, the copyright owner of the *White Album*. Capitol Records served Burton with a cease-and-desist order.

In protest, nearly 200 Web sites posted the *Grey Album*. In all, 100,000 downloads of the entire album were made, which in turn resulted in Capitol Records sending some of those sites cease-and-desist orders and requiring that they pay Capitol Records for illegal use of the music. Figure 6 summarizes the highlights of the Capitol Records' cease-and-desist letter.

FIGURE 6
Cease-and-desist letter summary

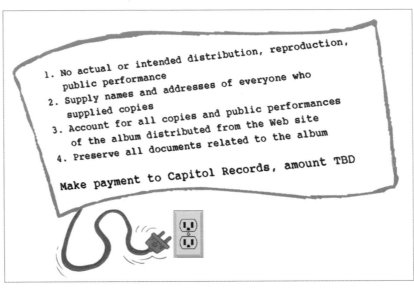

Exploring other legal resources

For a thorough overview of obtaining permission for various media, explore *Getting Permission: How to License and Clear Copyrighted Material Online and Off* by Richard Stim or visit Nolo Press at *www.nolo.com*. Nolo Press publishes several consumer-oriented legal titles, including books on the public domain. You can also check out Web-based resources such as FindLaw (*www.findlaw.com*), which contains articles and links on intellectual property in its For the Public section. The Chilling Effects Clearinghouse (*www.chillingeffects.com*) tracks and analyzes cease-and-desist notices. One of the foremost sites involved in cyberrights is the Electronic Frontier Foundation (*www.eff.org*). They are an excellent source of information about online freedom, online technologies (such as peer to peer), and censorship.

The epilogue to Mr. Burton's saga is that Capitol Records dropped legal proceedings after he signed a publishing contract with EMI, the parent company of Capitol records, and a producing contract with the band Gorillaz, who had signed with Virgin Records, an EMI label.

Acquiring Different Copyright Licenses

As you know, under copyright law, the copyright holder retains all rights to the work, which no one can violate without permission. However, you can easily retain your copyright while offering your work for use by others by licensing your work as **open access.**

QUICK**TIP**

Open access licenses by definition allow use, which is why the decision diagram shows a direct connection between Open Access and Use It. Naturally, some owners of open access licenses may have specific stipulations, such as no commercial use.

There are some sites on the Web that allow you to license your work as open access. One such site is Creative Commons, a nonprofit organization dedicated to building "a layer of reasonable, flexible copyright in the face of increasingly restrictive default rules." They base much of their philosophy on the original purpose of copyright law in the United States: to stimulate innovation. Figure 7 shows the Creative Commons home page. Note that once you designate a work in the public domain or open access, you cannot take it back or change it.

FIGURE 7
Creative Commons

As a complement to existing copyright law, Creative Commons developed a new set of licensing agreements—and the Web software to support their vision. Their site makes available someone's work for use (and often enhancement) by other people, but under conditions designated by the owner. The owner retains copyright and determines the breadth of use, which can range from public domain to more narrowly defined uses. The authors and artists who license their material with Creative Commons are self-selected—by definition, they share the organization's commitment to deepen and foster the public domain. The full set of Creative Commons licenses is summarized in Table 1. To obtain a license for material you would like to share, you simply fill out a form, as shown in Figure 8. One benefit of a Creative Commons license is its efficiency: you do not have to give individual permissions to everyone wanting to use your work. For a complete description of licenses and for further information about Creative Commons, visit *www.creativecommons.org*.

FIGURE 8

Choosing a Creative Commons license

Software automatically creates license and links for details

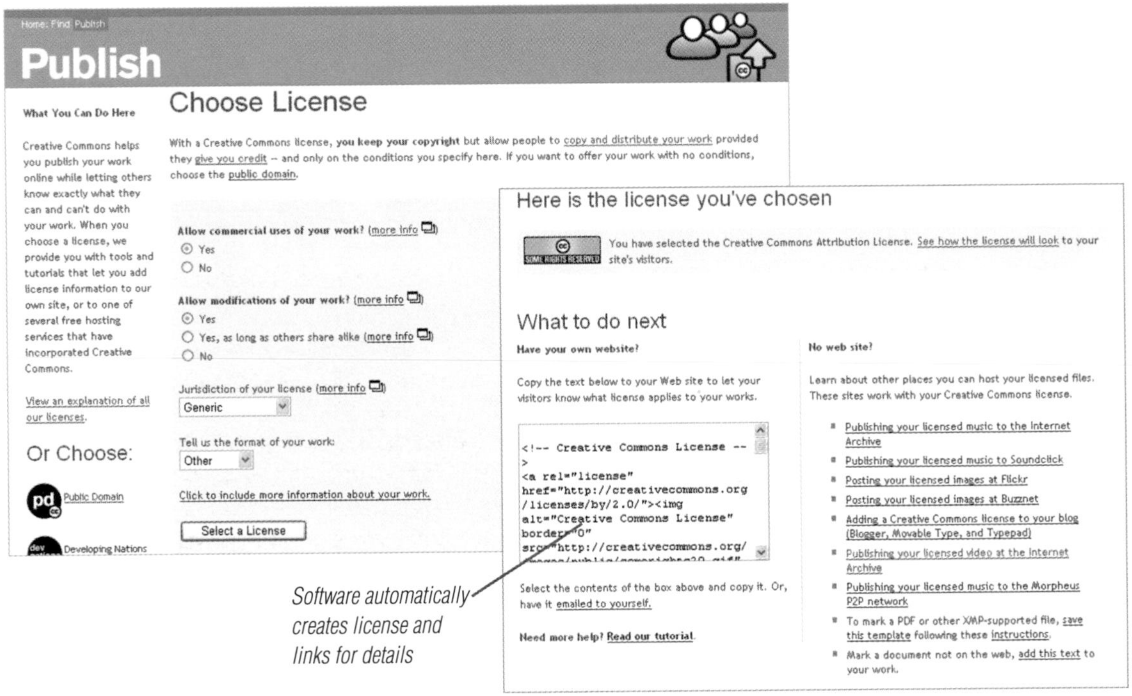

TABLE 1: Creative Commons Licences

symbol	specific type	name	summary of use
pd		Public Domain	Work can be freely reproduced, modified, etc., as any public domain work
fc		Founder's Copyright	Author retains copyright for 14 years, optional additional 14 years, then work enters public domain
cc		Creative Commons	Author retains copyright; works can be copied, displayed, and distributed in some manner
BY:		Attribution	Work can be distributed and altered; must credit you; commercial and noncommercial use
	BY: $ =	Attribution Noncommercial No Derivatives	Work can be distributed; must credit you; no alterations; noncommercial use
	BY: $ ↻	Attribution Noncommercial Share Alike	Work can be distributed and altered; must credit you; derivative work must carry same license; noncommercial use
	BY: $	Attribution Noncommercial	Work can be distributed and altered; must credit you; noncommercial use
	BY: =	Attribution No Derivatives	Work can be distributed; work cannot be altered; must credit you; commercial and noncommercial use
	BY: ↻	Attribution Share Alike	Work can be distributed and altered; must credit you; derivative work must carry same license; commercial and noncommercial use
⊕		Sampling	Pieces of work can be transformed; no advertising use; entire work cannot be copied or distributed
⊕		Sampling Plus	Pieces of work can be transformed; no advertising use; entire work can be copied or distributed for noncommercial purposes only
$		Noncommercial sampling Plus	Pieces of work can be transformed for noncommercial purposes only; entire work can be copied or distributed for noncommercial purposes only

Review terms of use

1. Connect to the Internet, navigate to the Online Companion, then click **Link 12**.

   The Animation Arthouse home page appears, as shown in Figure 9.

2. Scroll down to the third paragraph on the page, next to the Google ads, then read the terms of use.

   The terms are unambiguous and generous when you read them, although not easy to find or read.

3. Navigate to the Online Companion, click **Link 13**, then scroll down to view the terms of use.

   The morguefile.com home page fills the screen, as shown in Figure 10. Morguefile's terms allow commercial and noncommercial use.

4. Click **Image archive** in the list at the right, click the **Animals** category, then click **Pandas**.

   Thumbnail photos of pandas appear.

5. Click the **first thumbnail** in the top row, then compare your image to Figure 11.

   The photo fills the screen. At morguefile, the photographer can include a request to be informed when a photo is used.

6. Close your browser.

You reviewed the terms of use for two Web sites.

FIGURE 9
Terms of use

Terms

FIGURE 10
Photo-sharing terms of use

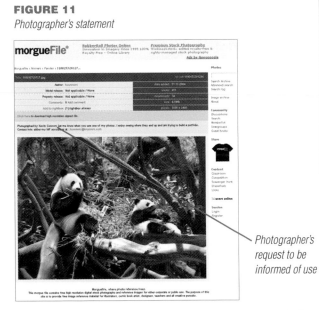

Your image
will vary

Terms

FIGURE 11
Photographer's statement

Photographer's
request to be
informed of use

UNDERSTAND
Media Files

 In this lesson, you will learn about file types for different media.

Understanding File Types

Content on the Web is available in a variety of file formats, including animation, audio, graphics, photographs, text, and video. Each type of media has formats designed specifically to support it. A **file format** is the way a software application encodes and structures data. A **file extension** identifies the file format of the specific software used to create the file.

The most common file format for photographs is the **JPEG (Joint Photographic Experts Group)** format. Generally, clip art, icons, and illustrations are supported in the **GIF (Graphics Interchange Format)** format. GIF files also support any image that requires a transparent background, such as a small animation embedded in a Web page, known as an *animated GIF*. Most of the photographs and other images in a Web page are **raster** or **bitmap** images, a file type that represents a picture as a matrix of pixels on a grid (resolution dependent). Bitmap images lose quality when resized or rescaled, as shown in Figure 12. Some download sites also offer **vector** files. Vector images have lines, known as paths, that can be edited and rescaled independently without losing image quality (resolution independent), as shown in Figure 13. Common graphic files and their extensions are listed in Table 2.

FIGURE 12
Enlarging a bitmap image

FIGURE 13
Enlarging a vector image

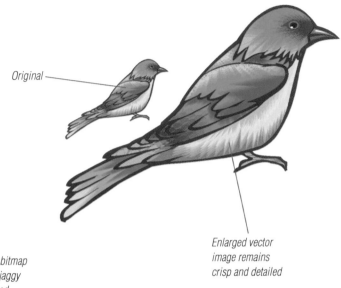

Original

Original bitmap image is sharp at that size

Enlarged bitmap image is jaggy and blurred

Enlarged vector image remains crisp and detailed

TABLE 2: Common Graphic File Extensions

name	extension	description
Bitmap	.bmp	Native Windows bitmap format
Encapsulated PostScript	.eps	Created and editable in an illustration or drawing program
Graphics Interchange Format	.gif	Best for drawings and illustrations
Joint Photographic Experts Group	.jpg, .jpeg, .jpe	Standard for compressed still images
Portable Networks Graphics	.png	Native Macromedia Fireworks format; bitmap graphics format
Tagged Image File Format	.tif, .tiff	Standard for high-quality still images; not viewable in a browser

Video captures images in full motion, while animation creates the illusion of movement by rapidly playing a series of still images in a sequence. You can integrate multiple file formats into a multimedia experience, which plays as a movie in your browser or on a CD or DVD. The terms *movie* and *multimedia* are often used interchangeably to describe rich content. Video or audio files on the Web are often referred to as **streaming video** or **streaming audio** because your browser does not have to completely download the file before playing it—it plays as it arrives (but after some data has been stored in a buffer). An example of streaming video is shown in Figure 14. Popular multimedia formats include SWF, **MOV (QuickTime Movie)**, **AVI (Audio Video Interleaved)**, and **MPEG (Motion Pictures Expert Group)**. See Table 3 for a more complete list of multimedia file extensions.

QUICKTIP

Some movie formats, such as AVI and MPEG, must be fully downloaded before they can play in a browser.

FIGURE 14
Streaming video (QuickTime)

Movie and audio playing

Current frame maker

Amount of movie already downloaded

Amount of movie to be downloaded

TABLE 3: Common Multimedia File Extensions

name	extension	description
Audio Video Interleaved	.avi	Native Windows video format; multiplatform
QuickTime Movie PostScript	.mov	Video and animation standard developed by Apple; multiplatform
Moving Picture Experts Group	.mpg, .mp2, .mp4	Digital video compression format and standards
Shockwave Flash	.swf	Flash content published on the Web
Windows Media Video	.wmv	Streaming video format developed by Microsoft

German scientist Karlheinz Brandenburg developed the first effective compression algorithms for audio, later dubbed MP3, in 1989. In 1996, he released an MP3 encoder and decoder, named L2ENC, along with its source code. The open source release initiated intense competition among electronics companies to produce better MP3 players, which ultimately benefited the consumer. Popular sound file formats are **AIF (Audio Interchange Format)**, **MP3 (Moving Pictures Expert Group Layer-3 Audio)**, and **WAV (Windows Wave)**. Table 4 lists file extensions for popular audio files.

QUICKTIP

The numbers that are included in the names of MPEG formats relate the order in which they were adopted as an industry standard by the Motion Pictures Experts Group.

TABLE 4: Common Audio File Extensions

name	extension	description
Advanced Audio Coding	.aac	Compressed format; Mac
Apple Computer Company	.acc	Compressed format; Mac
Audio Exchange File	.aif, .aiff	Uncompressed high-quality format; developed by Apple
Audio (Sun)	.au	Standard format for Java and Unix
Free Lossless Audio Codec	.flac	Open source; similar to MP3 in quality
Ogg Vorbis	.ogg	Greater capability than MP3; patent and royalty free
MPEG Layer 3 Audio	.mp3	Compressed format; multiplatform
Musical Instrument Digital Interface	.midi	Synthesized format (computer sounds)
RealAudio	.ra, .ram, .rm	Compressed high-quality format
Windows Wave	.wav	Uncompressed high-quality format; Windows native format
Window Media Audio	.wma	Windows format; copy protected

Understanding MP3 audio compression
The success of MP3 is a combination of an excellent compression algorithm and the range and peculiarities of human hearing. The compression algorithm incorporates psychoacoustics, the study of how the brain interprets audio, to dramatically reduce the size of sound files. Humans can hear in a range of 20–20,000 hertz (Hz). For comparison, other mammals such as elephants can hear as low as 1 Hz and bats can hear upwards of 120,000 Hz. Humans cannot adapt to hearing a soft or medium sound when a loud sound or sound with a similar frequency plays over it. The softer sound is literally drowned out, like when a plane flies low overhead and you're trying to listen to someone speak. The MP3 algorithm drops the sounds that we couldn't hear anyway, which reduces file size.

Understanding Optimization and Resolution

Before image or audio files can appear in a Web page, they are usually optimized for the Web. **Optimization** refers to selecting the file format that compresses the file so it can load quickly in your browser while maintaining image or audio quality.

Just as Web photos have been optimized for display on a computer monitor, the photos you view in print material have been saved in a format best suited for paper. The most important difference between the two is their resolution. **Resolution** refers to the degree of clarity and sharpness of a displayed or printed image. Higher resolution allows for more detail in an image; the more detail, the more you can enlarge the image until it appears grainy and loses quality. Screen images require considerably less resolution than print images, something you may have noticed if you've ever tried to print a low-resolution photo from the Web. This distinction can prove vital depending on your intended final use of the image you download.

Figure 15 shows an image at the same size but with a different number of pixels. If you download an image from a page on a Web site, its resolution is almost guaranteed to be low. However, sites dedicated to providing images for download, such as stock photography sites, offer them at higher resolution.

QUICKTIP

The standard resolution for Web images is 72 PPI (pixels per inch). Depending on the quality of your printer, the resolution of a print image can be as low as 180 PPI. Commercial printing can start at 300 PPI.

FIGURE 15

Comparing image resolution

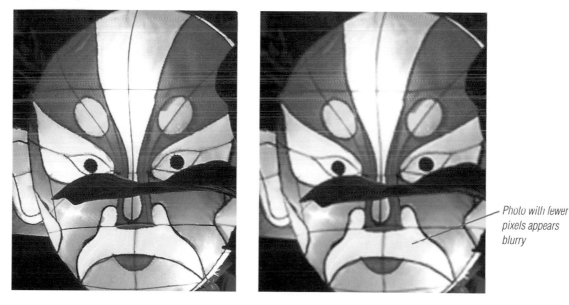

Photo with fewer pixels appears blurry

FIND CLIP ART
and Web Art

What You'll Learn

▶ *In this lesson, you will find clip art, assess its use for your purposes, and download clip art.*

Finding Clip Art and Web Art on the Web

The good news about clip art is that there is a lot of it available. The bad news is that much of it is for personal or educational use only and navigating to free sites can be grueling at times. Links to clip art became one of the earliest avenues for online marketing—it often involves going through intermediary sites (who have obviously optimized their sites to appear at the top of the search results of major search engines). These sites are often just portals to free and nonfree sites, but their adjunctive purpose is to bombard you with ads and cookies and send you through loops of repetitive navigation.

QUICK**TIP**

Also note that the same site can appear under different names and URLs, such as clipartconnection.com and clipart.com

Using Microsoft clip art

Owners of licensed Microsoft Office software can use clip art for personal or educational use, or for commercial use providing the clip art is not used in a logo and you do not resell the clip art in a collection. However, Microsoft cautions that the burden is on you to ascertain proper noncommercial use. From the company's perspective, your compliance is presumed when you clicked the End License User Agreement (EULA) check box that appears during the software-loading process. However, the courts' enforceability of the license, also known as a quick wrap license, is not guaranteed.

FIGURE 16

Clipart Connection home page

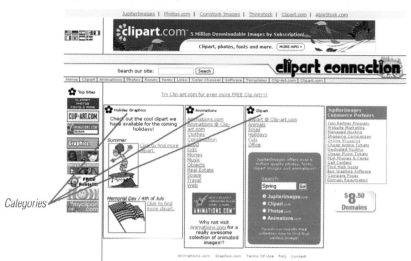

Categories

FIGURE 17

Turtle image ready for downloading

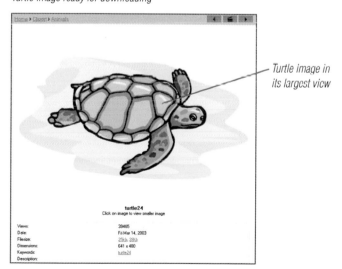

Turtle image in its largest view

1. Connect to the Internet, navigate to the Online Companion, then click **Link 14**.

   The Clipart Connection home page appears, as shown in Figure 16. Like many free clip art sites, the site is dominated by ads. The available categories are centered in the page.

2. Click **Animals** in the Clipart list, type **turtle** in the **Search** text box, then click **Search**.

   Assorted turtle clip art images appear on the page.

3. Click **turtle24** to display it, then click the **image** again to view it larger.

   The turtle image fills the screen, as shown in Figure 17. Downloading from the largest available view ensures the highest image quality.

   TIP If turtle24 does not appear on the page, click another turtle.

4. Right-click (Win) or ⌘-click (Mac) the **Image**, click **Save Picture As**, navigate to the drive and folder where your Data Files are stored, then click **Save**.

   The downloaded JPEG file is saved to your computer. The actual filename may vary from the image title.

   (continued)

5. Open a file management tool on your operating system (such as Windows Explorer, Mac Finder, or another program), adjust the settings to display extensions (if necessary), then navigate to the folder where you saved the image.

6. Preview **turtle24.jpg**.

> **TIP** In most file management programs, you can preview a file by right-clicking the filename, then clicking Preview in the shortcut menu.

7. Close the program used to preview the file, then close your file management program.

You searched for and downloaded clip art, then viewed the downloaded file on your computer.

Find animation

1. Click **Link 15** in the Online Companion.

   The Discovery Channel School Clip Art Gallery page appears.

2. Click **Copyright and Use Information** near the bottom of the page, and then review the Permission to Use Clip Art section.

   The site limits the number of downloads and restricts commercial use.

3. Return to the Clip Art Gallery page, then click **Animated Clips** in the Online Clip Art list.

   The Animated Clips page appears, as shown in Figure 18.

(continued)

FIGURE 18
Animated Clips page

Click link to view all animated clips on a single page

FIGURE 19
An animated clip

Animation changes color of text

4. Click **Next 12 images**, scroll down the page, then click the **empty head animation**.

   The empty head animation plays in the window, as shown in Figure 19.

5. Right-click (Win) or ⌘-click (Mac) the image, click **Save Picture As**, navigate to the drive and folder where your Data Files are stored, then click **Save**.

   The downloaded GIF file is saved to your computer. The actual filename may vary from the image title.

6. Open the file management tool that is on your operating system, then navigate to the folder where you saved the image.

7. Preview **ani-hello.gif**.

   The animation plays in your preview utility.

8. Close your file management tool and your browser.

You searched for and downloaded animated clip art, and then viewed the animation on your computer.

Understanding hotlinking bandwidth

Not following the rules a site has in place for using its content is rude and disrespectful at best, and devolves into a more serious offense if financial gain is involved or the copyright holder simply does not want their work used, ever. Even if you have permission to use a media file, you do not ever have the right to link directly to it from your Web page, in a practice known as **hotlinking bandwidth**, or leeching. More precisely, hotlinking occurs when you link to the other site's host server, which then supplies the bandwidth for the files to your site. The end result is that each time someone opens your Web page, you are tapping into the copyright owner's bandwidth to display the image, audio, or video, instead of using your own bandwidth. Web site hosts include instructions or software on how to prevent someone from hotlinking to a Web site. You can also use software to detect if someone has hotlinked to your site. Hotlinking bandwidth is considered an unauthorized download, which is a copyright infringement.

FIND Photographs

In this lesson, you will search for photos and examine their terms of use.

Finding Photographs on the Web

There will be times when you find the perfect photo for a project on a site that states "All Rights Reserved." When a copyright holder uses that phrase, they are not necessarily saying "Go away, this work is off-limits." But they are stating unequivocally that you must ask and receive permission before using the material. Chances are also that they would vigorously pursue any copyright infringement.

Perhaps more often, you will be lucky enough to find images whose owners plainly encourage their use. In any case, before downloading anything, always locate the terms of use and make sure you understand them, especially if you are seeking content for commercial use.

Universities and public libraries hold unique collections that have been digitized and placed on their Web sites. Many of the images may be in the public domain or have a relatively low fee associated with using them. For example, the University of Nebraska Press hosts a Gallery of the Open Frontier. They scanned thousands of images at high resolution from the National Archives that pertain to the American West. The Portraits section of the Gallery of the Open Frontier collection is shown in Figure 20. In addition, leading public libraries, such as the New York Public Library, have already digitized hundreds of thousands of photos and images of their vast holdings. In addition, photomuse.org, a collaboration of the George Eastman House and the International Center of Photography in Midtown Manhatten, is digitizing 200,000 masterwork photographs in searchable databases.

Beyond government and commercial sources lies what could become the bedrock of file access: sites hosted by individuals who foster sharing media. These sites can contain media created solely by the host, collections of material compiled by the host, or files posted by hundreds of individuals who want to share their work.

The baseline agreement is to permit personal use, and it only goes up from there. For example, stock.xchng, shown in Figure 21, states that "You may use any of the photos in our system free of charge for any commercial or personal design work if you obey the specified restrictions concerning each photo you download. You are not allowed to use any of the images found herein for the purpose of spreading hate or discrimination, or to defame or victimize other people, societies, or cultures."

Understanding Blogs

One effective means to communicate about ideas, such as using media, is through blogs. The Internet is intrinsically dynamic—in both the conventional and computer-based definitions of the term. It is in a state of constant change or motion and actions or content change frequently. Blogs reflect and embody this notion. A **blog** (short for weblog) is an online journal that includes entries on a topic and links to other articles. Critical analysis of all blogs centers around their accuracy and whether authors should be granted the constitutional protections afforded to journalists.

FIGURE 20
University collection

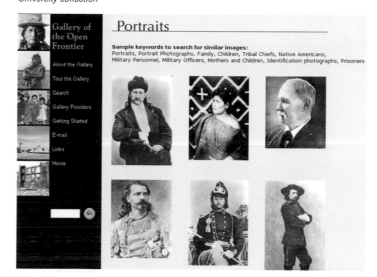

FIGURE 21
Public photo-sharing site

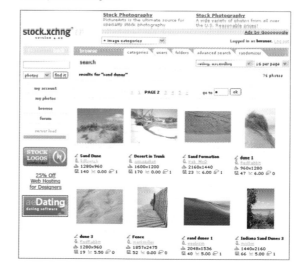

Photoblogs replace text with photographs, although many photoblogs include captions and welcome comments. A sample photoblog is shown in Figure 22. Blogs can be read-only, interactive, or they can allow readers to publicly comment or rate entries. The range of topics is diverse and expansive, including personal diaries, philosophical musings, political, news, entertainment, and so on. Note that photos posted on a photoblog are probably not in the public domain, and the photographer may not allow any downloads. Several software packages or services are available for creating blogs.

QUICK**TIP**

Bloggers who wish to remain anonymous can use software that hides the IP address from host services. This is valuable if the user is blogging from a company computer.

Understanding RSS Feeds

Blogs and the latest news from Web sites can be syndicated and distributed Web-wide using a method known as **Rich Site Summary** or **Really Simple Syndication (RSS)**. RSS is considered an effective way of managing information overload. Instead of clicking several sites to locate and read information of interest to you, RSS software brings the headlines to you via XML.

RSS uses a Web standard known as **Extensible Markup Language (XML)** to transmit the latest content from various Web sites without you ever needing to

FIGURE 22
Photoblog

Photographing art in museums

Photographing any privately held work of art without permission infringes on the copyright owner's rights. Even if the art is on public display, such as at a gallery or museum, the artist's copyright is still protected. If the work on display is in the public domain, you are legally within your rights to photograph it. But, once you enter the museum or gallery, you are also bound by the rules of the facility. So, just as they can prohibit smoking, food, or beverages, they can also prohibit photography.

navigate to the site. RSS headlines appear with hyperlinks and summaries. You can download feeds from several sites based on your professional or personal interests. You can also share material on or from your own Web site. You can read RSS content by downloading a reader, known as an **aggregator**. Once your browser or e-mail program is set up to read RSS feeds, you can navigate to sites that offer RSS feeds and then subscribe to that feed. Figure 23 shows sample RSS feeds in a browser.

QUICK**TIP**

RSS was originally created by Netscape.

Understanding Podcasting

Just as an RSS aggregator transmits visual content to your browser, podcasting transmits audio files that are playable on a portable MP3 device, such as an iPod. Podcasts are individually recorded programs, such as news, music, travel guides, and all manner of content eclectic. Unlike radio or streaming audio, you can listen to podcasts whenever you wish. You simply subscribe to a podcast of interest, and the device's software downloads episodes automatically. You can also listen to podcasts on your computer.

Using Government Resources

State government Web sites and the legal status of images on them varies widely between states. Be prepared to drill well into a site before you find copyright information, and note that it may change from agency to agency. Also check associated state Web sites, such as state historical societies and state libraries.

All work created by federal employees in the course of their employment is in the public domain. However, not all government work is performed by federal employees; much third-party content, including work created by government contractors, is protected by copyright. Some notable exceptions are where all or the majority of images are in the public domain, such as those created by departments and agencies such as NASA, the Department of

FIGURE 23
Sample RSS feeds

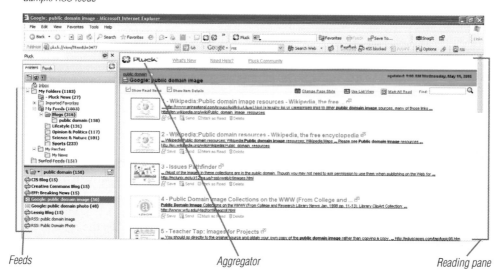

Feeds   Aggregator   Reading pane

Agriculture, the National Park Service, and the Fish and Wildlife Service, shown in Figure 24. For example, all space flight photos are in the public domain, and images taken by satellites and other spacecraft are usually just attributable to their sponsor, such as a joint effort between a university and agency flight center.

One thing to keep in mind when searching for government media is that they often were created for specific research or programs. They may not be particularly well composed or of high resolution, though many are. Photos may be divided throughout the site based on a specific research program, so extensive surfing may be necessary.

Even though most government images are available to use, that does not mean that you do not still have to credit the photo. Generally, government sites, especially NASA, are fairly clear about how you should give credit.

Restricting Image Content

The large search engines allow you to filter the content of your search results. There may be a variety of reasons why you would want to eliminate explicit images from your search results: work or school policies, inappropriate viewing by others, or you know that those images are not relevant to your search.

You can specifically filter your results to purge explicit images by clicking options on the advanced search page or preferences

page of a search engine. Figure 25 shows Dogpile's filtering option. You should read the FAQ or About Us sections for the policies of

FIGURE 24
Government image source

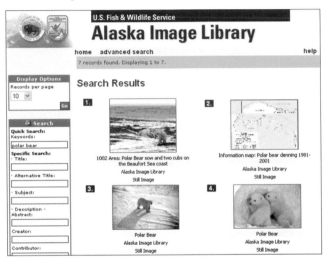

sites that support image sharing, such as Flickr.com or FreeFoto.com.

FIGURE 25
Image filter

FIGURE 26

PD Photo.org home page

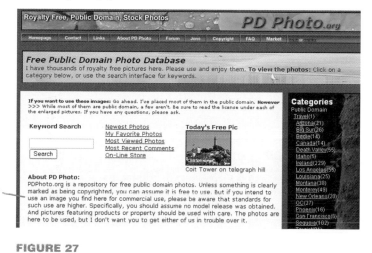

Site states terms of use on home page

FIGURE 27

Keyword photo search results

Terms of use added to each search page

Find public domain photos

1. Navigate to the Online Companion, then click **Link 16**.

   The PD Photo.org home page appears, as shown in Figure 26.

2. Read the paragraphs at the top of the page about using the image, then click **Copyright** on the navigation bar.

3. Review the information, then click **Homepage** on the navigation bar.

   While the host clearly indicates that his intent is to provide public domain images, he also cautions that some images have copyright protection and guesses against using images of people without a model release.

   TIP Using photos of private property, events, attractions, and so on also require a release, especially if you are going to use them commercially.

4. Type **cave** in the Keyword Search text box, then click **Search**.

   Photos matching the keyword appear, as shown in Figure 27.

   (continued)

5. Click the first **Crystal Cave** photo in the results, then compare your screen to Figure 28.

6. Read the licensing information for the image by clicking the **Public Domain** link, then use your browser's **Back button** to return to the page when you have read it.

> **TIP** If the crystal cave photo does not appear on the page, click another cave photo.

7. Save the image.

You searched for public domain images, reviewed the terms of use, and downloaded the image.

Find photos with mixed licensing

1. Navigate to the Online Companion, then click **Link 17**.

The Flickr home page appears, as shown in Figure 29. Flickr is a free photo-sharing service that allows users to store, sort, search, and share photos online. It supports its members using Creative Commons licenses. Like other photo-sharing sites, members have more privileges than visitors. Some sites only allow members to download photos or give members the option to not display their work to visitors.

(continued)

FIGURE 28
Selected photo

License information

FIGURE 29
Flickr home page

Free account link

FIGURE 30

Flickr search results

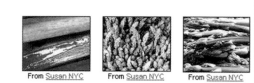

Tags / ediblestalks

You're looking at all the
public photos tagged with
ediblestalks.

From Susan NYC   From Susan NYC   From Susan NYC

FIGURE 31

An image and its information

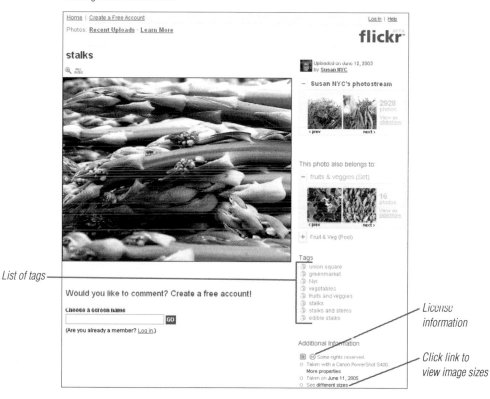

List of tags

License information

Click link to view image sizes

2. Type **edible stalks** in the Find a photo of text box, then press **[Enter]** (Win) or **[Return]** (Mac).

   Photos matching *edible stalks* appear, as show in Figure 30. Because new photos are constantly added to Flickr, your list may vary.

3. Click the **picture of horizontal asparagus stalks** (if available), then compare your screen to Figure 31. (If it is not available, click a different image.)

   Artists can attach **tags** to their photos, which are keywords that identify one of any number of categories the artist has selected for the photo. You can easily use tags to cross-reference your work. The license that the artist has chosen for the photo also appears on the page, making it easy to ascertain its status. You can also choose the size of the image you want to download.

4. Click the **Attribution-ShareAlike License icon** under Additional Information, review the license and the number of search results in both searches, then note duplicates, if any.

You searched for a phrase and then compared search results.

Search a government site for public domain photos

1. Navigate to the Online Companion, then click **Link 18**.

   The Hubble home page opens, as shown in Figure 32.

2. Click **GALLERY** in the navigation bar at the top, then click **PICTURE ALBUM**.

3. Click **STARS**, then roll over the thumbnails until you see **Chandra/HST X-Ray/Optical Composite**, as shown in Figure 33.

   Thumbnail photos in the Star Collection appear. The text that appears when you position the mouse pointer over an image is known as **alternate text**, or **alt text**.

4. Click the **Chandra/HST X-Ray/Optical Composite thumbnail**.

5. Read the Image Credit section, click **copyright** at the bottom of the page, then review the Copyright Notice.

You searched a government site for images and reviewed the copyright terms.

FIGURE 32
Hubble home page

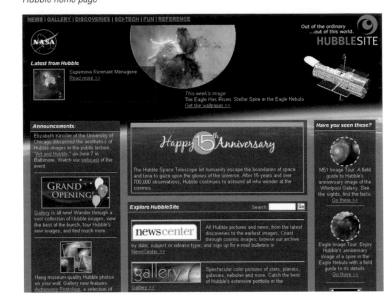

FIGURE 33
Alt text in a thumbnail

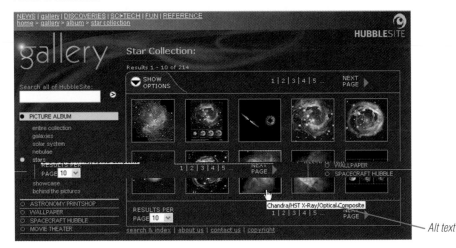

— *Alt text*

FIND
Video

In this lesson, you will search for video files.

Finding Movie Files

You can find a surprisingly large amount of video on the Internet, but if the source is unknown (as it often is with video files), you probably cannot use it. Using pirated movie content is never a good idea. Major film studios have been relentless in their pursuit and prosecution of movie pirates and distributors. It is also a criminal offense to have a movie on your computer that has not yet been released.

Finding stock movies is easy thanks to The Internet Archive. They work with the Library of Congress and the Smithsonian Institution and have placed online thousands of books and audio files. They also offer a wide variety of video donated under open source licenses. Movie Entertainment OnLine hosts several dozen movies that have migrated into the public domain. Of course, if your needs are specific or the need for quality is important, you can buy snippets from stock video suppliers.

Advancing digital preservation

Many of the efforts for cultural preservation have centered on digitizing old movies and recordings, and deservedly so. The Library of Congress is coordinating a national digital preservation strategy. Millions of digital materials with "research or cultural value" have been lost from the early days of the Internet as a result of inadequate storage and the obsolescence of dozens of file formats. Several universities have been selected as partners in the preservation effort, known as "Preserving Our Digital Heritage: Plan for the National Digital Information Infrastructure and Preservation Program."

Find video

1. Navigate to the Online Companion, then click **Link 19**.

   The Internet Archive home page appears, as shown in Figure 34.

2. Type **duck and cover** in the Search text box, click the **All Media Types list arrow**, click **Moving Images**, then click **GO**.

3. Click **Duck and Cover**, the first highlighted entry at the top of the page, then compare your screen to Figure 35.

   Information about the film, reviews, and viewing options appear. Each movie also has an animated GIF preview of selected frames.

4. View the movie in the format of your choice, or click **View thumbnails** if you are unable to watch the movie.

   You searched for and viewed a public domain movie.

FIGURE 34
Internet Archive home page

Media categories

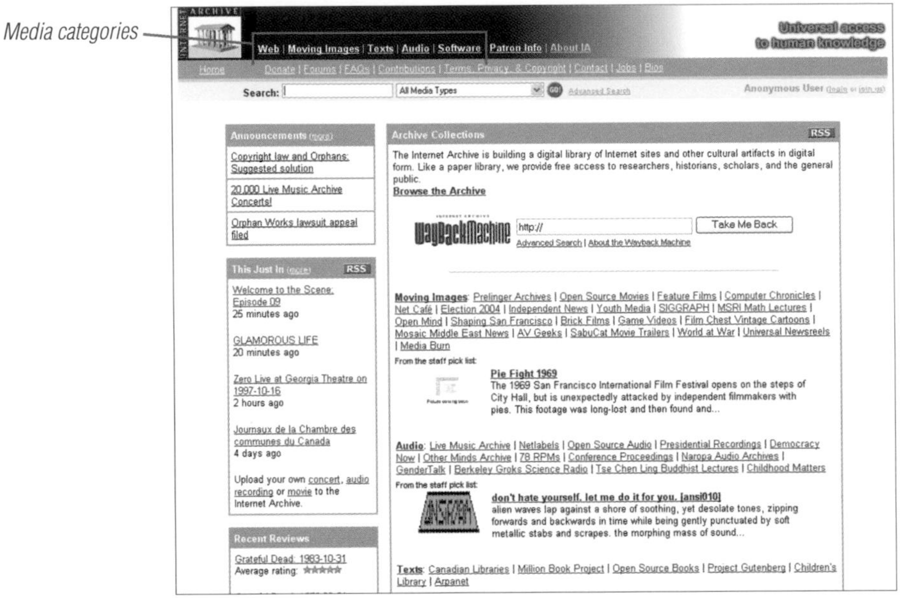

FIGURE 35
Duck and Cover page

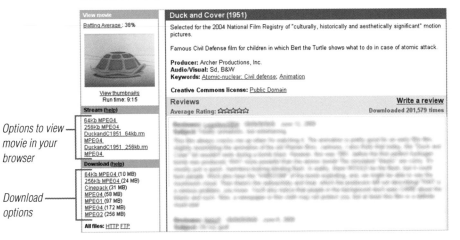

Options to view movie in your browser

Download options

FIND
Audio

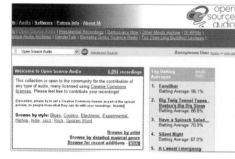

 In this lesson, you will search for audio files

Finding Audio Files

Your audio needs can vary widely. You may want to insert sound in an online slide presentation or multimedia project, or you may want to insert sound directly in your Web page for buttons or rollovers. Sound bits from popular songs, movies, and television shows are plentiful on the Web. Many have just been recorded off the medium of origin, which makes their usability open to question. Note that for music, however, copyright can be established by the value of a song.

While it may be proper to apply the fair use doctrine to your use of audio files, remember that actions such as denying credit to the artist, profiting from its use, or claiming that its purpose is for entertainment purposes only may not serve you well as your defense in court.

QUICKTIP

Bootlegging a recording from a live performance is considered copyright infringement, even if the performance was not otherwise fixed in a tangible medium.

Find sound effects

1. Navigate to the Online Companion, then click **Link 20**.

   The A1 Free Sound Effects home page appears, as shown in Figure 36.

2. Click **Free Sound Effects**, click **Radio**, then review the terms of use beneath the radio image.

3. Scroll down the page to the Most Popular Downloads section shown in Figure 37, then click **Heartbeat**.

   The sound clip plays in your computer's default media player.

4. Scroll down the page to the Other Sound Downloads section, then click **Censored Beep**.

You searched for and played a sound clip.

FIGURE 36
A1 Free Sound Effects home page

FIGURE 37
Download sections

Heartbeat clip

FIGURE 38

Open Source Audio page

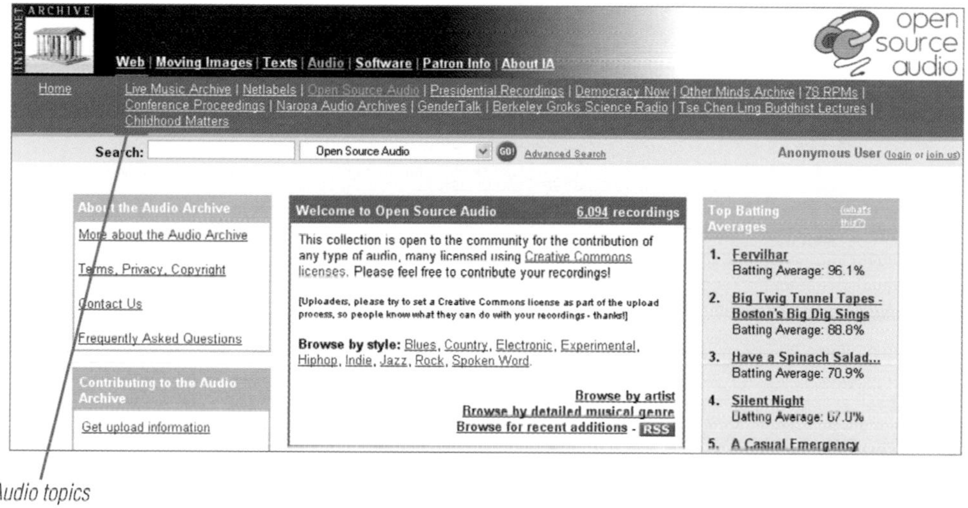

Audio topics

Find music

1. Navigate to the Online Companion, click **Link 19**, click **Audio** in the navigation bar, then click **Open Source Audio** beneath the navigation bar.

   The Internet Archive Open Source Audio page appears, as shown in Figure 38.

2. Click **Hiphop** in the Welcome to Open Source Audio section, then click **Electronic Hiphop** in the Browse Hip-Hop section.

   Links to various artists appear.

   (continued)

3. If necessary, scroll down the page, then click **Get Serious**.

   Information about the song appears, as shown in Figure 39. Several file formats are available for download, or you can play the song as streaming audio.

   > **TIP** If the Get Serious link is not visible, type Get Serious in the Search text box, then click Go.

4. Click the **Creative Commons logo** in the The Recording box at the left, review the license type, then close the Creative Commons window.

5. Click **Lo-Fi** as the Stream option in the The Recording box at the left.

   The song plays in your default media player.

6. Listen to all or part of the song, close your media player, then close your browser.

You searched for and played public domain music.

FIGURE 39
Song information

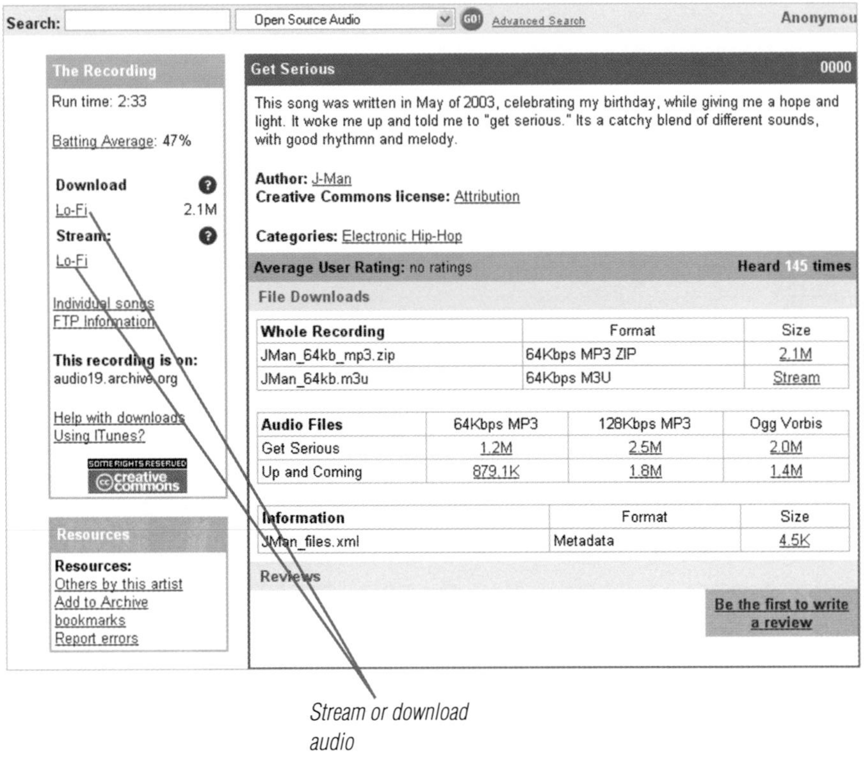

Stream or download audio

FIND MEDIA AT
the Library of Congress

▶ In this lesson, you will learn about finding media on government sites and search for media at the Library of Congress.

Understanding the Library of Congress

The Library of Congress is the world's largest library. Although it was originally conceived as the legislative library for Congress—no one from the general public was allowed in—it has evolved to be the de facto national library. The Library of Congress was one of the first government agencies to go online and one of the last to upgrade its database search system from the early Telnet system. Over 10 percent of its 130 million holdings are photographs or recordings, much of which is in the public domain.

QUICK**TIP**

The Library of Congress did not receive funding for its first dedicated building until the 1870s. A major factor for funding was due to the onslaught of printed materials created as a result of the Copyright Act of 1870, which relegated copyright registration and deposit activities to the Library.

Navigating the Library of Congress

Because the Library of Congress site contains voluminous content, searching it can be frustrating. Some of the most user-friendly pages of the site are the collections pages. For example, the Library has compiled hundred of different topics in the American Memory series, some of which are shown in Figure 40. The advantage of browsing collections is that you access all media types, and they are designed specifically for the Web. The Library also offers virtual tours of current exhibits, but the content may not all be online

You can specifically search for photos and other images, video, and sound in their respective databases. However, because not all of the Library's holding are digitized or online, you may locate the item you want only to discover it's available to you only if you visit the Library of Congress in Washington, DC.

National Archives

The National Archives and Records Division, more commonly known as the National Archives, houses millions of documents and images "created by those who participated in or witnessed" American history. For example, the National Archives is the custodian of material in presidential libraries. The majority of its holdings are also in the public domain. The easiest way to search for downloadable media in the archives is through the Archival Research Catalog (ARC), a searchable database of digitalized photos, movies and video, sound, and so on. You can explore the National Archives at *www.archives.gov.*

FIGURE 40
Samples from the American Memory collection

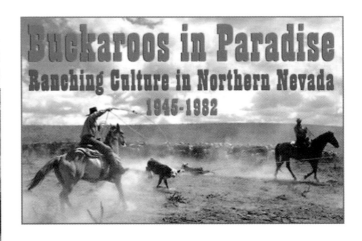

FIGURE 41
Library of Congress home page

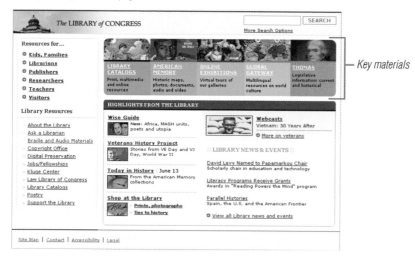

Key materials

Find photos at the Library of Congress

1. Connect to the Internet, navigate to the Online Companion, then click **Link 21**.

   The Library of Congress home page appears, as shown in Figure 41.

2. Click **AMERICAN MEMORY** at the top of the page, click **Cities**, **Towns** in the Browse box, then click **Panoramic Photographs — 1851–1991**.

3. Click **bridges** in the Overview paragraph.

   A list of bridges appears, as shown in Figure 42. You passed several other collections as you drilled down to this page.

   (continued)

FIGURE 42
Bridges topic

Web page path

Click link to display thumnails

Extensive collection-related resources

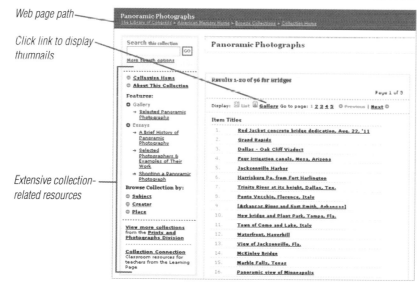

4. Click number 11, **Town of Como and Lake, Italy**.

   The copyright was created in 1910, as shown in Figure 43. Copyright law specifies that copyrights in works first published or copyrighted before January 1, 1923, have expired.

5. Click the **picture** to view the enlarged image.

   A larger version of the photo appears along with a link to download an uncompressed version.

6. Return to the American Memory page.

You searched for a photo in the American Memory collection in the Library of Congress.

FIGURE 43
Photo and information

Result 11 of 96 for Bridges

Back to Results list   ⊙ **Previous Item** | **Next Item** ⊙

Panoramic Photographs
Click on picture for larger image, full item, or more versions

Rights and Reproductions

Collection-specific copyright and copying information

Town of Como and Lake, Italy.

Created/Published
c1910.

Notes
Copyright deposit; Notman Photo Co.; March 21, 1910.
Copyright claimant's address: Boston.
No. 70.

Subjects
Railroad bridges.
Mountains.
Cityscape photographs.
Panoramic photographs.
Gelatin silver prints.
Italy--Como.

Photo-specific copyright information

Related Names
Notman Photo Co., copyright claimant.

Medium
1 photographic print : gelatin silver ; 10 x 42 in.

Call Number
PAN FOR GEOG - Italy no. 23

Part of
Panoramic photographs (Library of Congress)

Repository
Library of Congress Prints and Photographs Division Washington, D.C. 20540 USA

Digital ID
(**digital file from intermediary roll film copy**) pan 6a22961 http://hdl.loc.gov/loc.pnp/pan.6a22961

FIGURE 44

Viewing the Browse Collections page

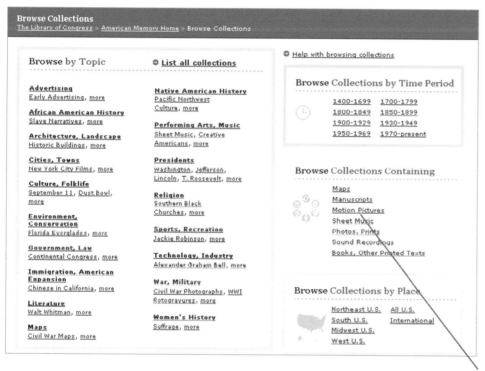

Click Motion
Pictures

1. Verify that the American Memory page in the Library of Congress home page is open.

2. Click **More browse options** at the bottom of the Browse Collections by Topic section, then click **Motion Pictures** in the Browse Collections Containing section at the right, as shown in Figure 44.

   The Motion Pictures collections page appears.

3. Click the fifth entry, Film, **Animated ~ 1900–1921**, then read the introductory paragraph about the films.

   The Origins of American Animation page appears.

(continued)

4. Click **Alphabetical Title List**, then click **Fun in a bakery shop**.

   The information and link page appears.

   | **TIP** This was an early protoanimation film and was shot using a stop-motion claymation technique.

5. Play the video in the format of your choice, pause the player in scenes you like, as shown in Figure 45, then close the player.

6. Close your browser.

You searched for a video in the American Memory collection in the Library of Congress.

FIGURE 45
Frames from the movie

Match each term with the statement that best describes it.

_____ 1. Bitmap image

_____ 2. AVI

_____ 3. royalty-free

_____ 4. RSS

_____ 5. photoblog

_____ 6. open access

_____ 7. terms of use

_____ 8. MP3

a. Permission assumed for use of a work, but some conditions may apply

b. Unlimited or unrestricted use of a work following payment

c. An online application that contains periodic postings of images

d. A video file format.

e. The rules that govern how a copyrighted work may be used

f. An audio file format

g. A format for syndicating online content

h. An image represented by pixels on a grid

Select the best answer from the list of choices.

9. Which of the following is characteristic of a licensing agreement?
   a. Copyright owners must post a link to one
   b. It is legally binding
   c. If you don't see one, you can use the work as you wish
   d. It is always for one-time use

10. What is an aggregator used for?
    a. To optimize a bitmap image
    b. To compress audio files
    c. To syndicate online content
    d. To copyright online content

11. Which term best describes alt text?
    a. The text accompanying a photoblog
    b. Terms of use that have open access
    c. Search criteria at the Library of Congress
    d. Text that appears when you move the mouse over an image

12. Which of the following would be characteristic of an exclusive license?
    a. The work cannot be used at all.
    b. Anyone can use the work as long as the copyright owner is given attribution
    c. The work can be used for two weeks on a billboard in Times Square
    d. One-time use by a tax-exempt nonprofit organization

13. Which the following is not considered part of a multimedia file?
    a. Sound
    b. Search results
    c. Video
    d. Animation

Understand licenses and permissions.

1. Using your favorite word-processing program, save a document as **Resolution** in the drive and folder where you are saving files for this book, then explain the difference between exclusive and non-exclusive rights.
2. List three kinds of terms of use.
3. Describe the complexity involved in wanting to use copyrighted multimedia.
4. Describe what Creative Commons does.
5. Connect to the Internet, navigate to the Online Companion, then click Link 19.
6. Type **copyright** in the Search text box, click the All Media Types list arrow, scroll down to the bottom, then click FAQs.
7. Click GO, then read the summaries of the search results

Understand media files.

1. Using your favorite word-processing program, describe how resolution affects online and print images differently.
2. Explain how playing streaming video or audio differs from playing down-loaded media.
3. Save and close the Resolution document.

Find clip art and Web art.

1. Navigate to the Online Companion, then click Link 22.
2. Click Fantasy/Medieval in the Cartoon Clip Art section, then click Dragon2 in the first row.
3. Right-click (Win) or ⌘-click (Mac) the image, navigate to the drive and folder where your Data Files are stored, then save the file.
4. Preview the file using the file management tool on your computer.
5. Navigate to the Online Companion, then click Link 23.

6. Scroll down the page, then click Click here for a clickable list of animations.
7. Click the sixth entry, Egyptian Couple stroll past an obelisk.
8. Save the file to the folder where your Data Files are stored.
9. Play the animation using the file management tool on your computer.

Find photographs.

1. Navigate to the Online Companion, then click Link 24.
2. Click Advanced search beneath the search text box.
3. Type **lava lamp** in the search words text box, then click Submit.
4. Click the close up of the yellow lava bubbles photo, then read the terms of use beneath the photo.
5. Navigate to the Online Companion, then click Link 25.
6. Type **kangaroo and joey** in the search text box, then click find it.
7. Click the Joey in the pouch photo, then read the artist's terms of use beneath the photo. (*Hint*: Click another photo if necessary.)
8. Navigate to the Online Companion for this book, then click Link 26.
9. Click Site Overview in the navigation bar, read the Releases section, then return to the Index page.
10. Click the Select a Park list arrow, click Big Cypress National Preserve, click GO, then Click the first photo (BICY1059.PCD) to review it.

Find video.

1. Navigate to the Online Companion, then click Link 19.
2. Type **day the earth stood still** in the Search text box, click the All Media Types list arrow, click SabuCat Movie Trailers, then click GO!
3. Play the movie in the format of your choice, compare your screen to the frame shown in Figure 46. (*Hint*: The first several seconds are black.)
4. Close your player.

Find sound.

1. Navigate to the Online Companion then click Link 27.
2. Scroll to the Public Domain Sound Effects section, then click Domestic Sounds.
3. Click spray.wav, then click knock.wav.
4. Close your media browser.
5. Navigate to the Online Companion for this book, then click Link 28.
6. Click Ragtime Piano Music, then click Scott Joplin on the Maple Leaf Rag.
7. Listen to all or part of the song, then close your media player.

Find media at the Library of Congress.

1. Navigate to the Online Companion, then click Link 21.
2. Click Researchers in the Resources for section, then click Research Centers in the Research Tools on this Site section (at the right).
3. Click Prints & Photographs in the Special Formats and Genre section.
4. Click Prints & Photographs Online Catalog in the Trying to Find a Picture? section (at the left).
5. Click People in the Want to see some samples? section.
6. Scroll down, then click Portrait of Marianne Anderson.
7. Compare your screen to Figure 47, then close your browser.

FIGURE 46
Completed Skills Review (1)

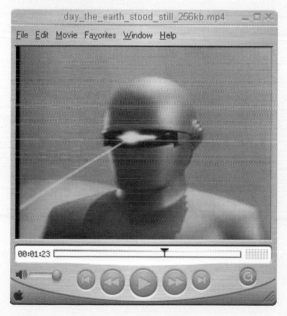

FIGURE 47
Completed Skills Review (2)

Your favorite local public radio program is trying something new during pledge week. Instead of the usual barrage of solicitations for coffee mugs, you've volunteered to help produce a comedic radio theater segment, Now Listen Slowly. Two of the characters, Barren Mind and Lois Carmen Denominator, are astronauts lost in space. One of your jobs is to locate several sounds for those scenes. The other is to find space photos to use in publicity flyers. You'll hunt the Internet for great media, making sure that the media can be used for this purpose.

1. Create a folder named **Now Listen Slowly** in the drive and folder where you are saving files for this book.
2. Connect to the Internet, then navigate to the Online Companion and the Surf and Turf Index of Online Resources.
3. Using the Surf and Turf Index as a resource, locate and download at least six sounds from at least three different sites that fit the space theme or are ominous and that are licensed for personal, noncommercial, or educational use. Check out links from this chapter or in the Sound section of the Master Table. (*Hint*: Look for computer, rocket, science fiction, or electronic sounds.)
4. Locate and download at least four photos that fit the space theme. In addition to the Images section in the Surf and Turf Index, you can use links you learned about in this chapter. (*Hint*: Look for the following words in the Web Site Owner column of the Index: earth, science, hubble, space, planetary, and satellite.)
5. Open a program that supports image and sound files, then create a file named **Now Listen Slowly**. (*Hint*: For Word, click Insert on the menu bar, click Object, click Create from File, then browse to the sound file. For PowerPoint, click Insert on the menu bar, click Movies and Sounds, click Sounds from File, then browse to the sound file. For other programs, consult the online help system or ask your instructor if you need help.)
6. Insert the image and sound files using a layout of your choice.
7. Compare your file to the sample shown in Figure 48.
8. Save the Now Listen Slowly file, then close it.

FIGURE 48
Sample Completed Project Builder 1

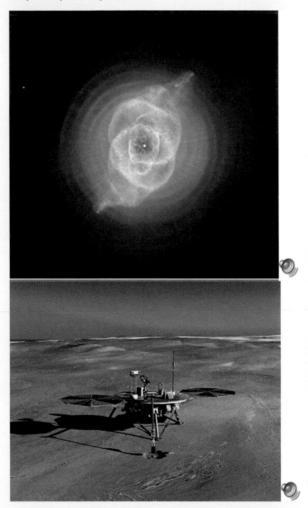

One of your coworkers sent you a link to a photoblog, and you spent your lunch hour viewing the photos. You planned to download your favorite photo to use as your desktop wallpaper, when you noticed that there were no terms of use listed on the blog. Because you know copyright is implicit, you didn't download the photo but instead decided to help the blogger add terms of use to their site. You decide to research other blogs and photo-sharing sites for terms of use, so that you can provide the blogger with examples.

1. Create a folder named **Best of Blog** in the drive and folder where you are saving files for this book.
2. Open your favorite word-processing program, then save a new document named **Best of Blog**.
3. Connect to the Internet, navigate to your favorite search engine, then search for "best photoblogs."
4. Open several sites that include links to photoblogs.
5. Navigate to several "best of" photoblogs, then copy the terms of use and the site's URL into the Best of Blog document.
6. Review the terms of use, navigate to three sites whose photos are in the public domain or have a license that permits downloading for personal, noncommercial, or educational use, then download a photo you like from each site. (*Hint*: If you don't have three sites that fit the criteria, go back and search for more.)
7. Determine a favorite photo, then if desired, insert the photo next to its parent photoblog name in the Best of Blog document.
8. Save your changes to the Best of Blog document, compare your image to the sample shown in Figure 49, then close the document.

FIGURE 49
Sample Completed Project Builder 2

http://www.frangipani.info/gallery/

Attribution-NonCommercial-NoDerivs

Noncommercial: You may not use this work for commercial purposes.

No Derivative Works: You may not alter, transform, or build upon this work.

* For any reuse or distribution, you must make clear to others the license terms of this work.

* Any of these conditions can be waived if you get permission from the copyright holder.

Aggregator
Software that allows individuals to subscribe to online feeds.

AIF
Audio Interchange Format.

Alt text *or* **Alternate text**
The text that appears as a caption when a mouse hovers over an image.

Archie
An early Internet search engine developed at McGill University.

ARPA
Advanced Research Projects Agency.

Attribution
The right of the author of a work to claim ownership and recognition for the work.

Author
The creator or owner of a copyrighted work.

Avatar
An online graphical representation of a person.

AVI
Audio Video Interleaved.

Bandwidth
The amount of data a digital connection can transmit in a set amount of time, usually measured in seconds.

Berne Convention
An international treaty giving foreign authors reciprocal copyright protection.

Bitmap
A picture represented by a matrix of pixels on a grid—resolution dependent.

Blog
An online journal, usually written by one person and sometimes open to commentary.

Boolean operators
Logical mathematical operators you can use to construct complex searches.

Bot
Any computer program that performs a recursive function.

Clustering
Search results grouped around a theme.

Contributory infringement
When a person directly contributes to the direct infringement of someone's intellectual property.

Copyright-free
Same as royalty-free; often incorrectly construed to mean in the public domain.

Copyright infringement
Unauthorized use of copyrighted material that violates a copyright owner's exclusive rights.

Copyright law
An exclusive right granted to authors to control certain aspects of their work.

CPU
Central processing unit.

Crawler
Specific bot that follows each hyperlink to find incidence of keywords; *same as* spider.

Dead link
Hyperlink to an obsolete or nonexistent Web page.

Derivative work
The right of the author to recast, transform, or adapt an original work.

Design patent
Protects the overall ornamentative appearance of an object.

Digital watermark
Embedded code in a media file or transmission that identifies the work.

Directory
Human-selected database for searching.

DNS
Domain name server.

Domain name
The text equivalent of an IP address.

Dynamic database
Content created on the fly in response to user input.

Exclusive
A license whose use is granted to a single user under specific conditions.

Fair use
Allows limited use of copyrighted materials without permission of the copyright holder.

GIF
Graphics Interchange Format.

Gopher
Early successful Internet search engine.

GUI
Graphical user interface.

Head
The top of an HTML page.

Hotlinking bandwidth
Stealing a Web site's bandwidth by directly linking to media on another site from your own.

HTML
HyperText Markup Language.

HTTP
HyperText Transfer Protocol.

Index
A type of database built on keywords and ranking.

Index search engine
A type of search index based on spider-located entries and ranking.

Intangible asset
An asset without physical substance.

Integrity
The right of authors to prevent use of their names if the work is distorted or significantly altered.

Intellectual property
A creative product of the human mind.

Invisible Web
Public resources of data and information not usually searchable by search engines.

IP
Internet protocol.

IP address
Unique four-digit string Web site identifier.

ISP
Internet Service Provider.

JPEG
Joint Photographic Experts Group.

Keyword
Significant word or phrase used to search Web pages.

Kbps
Kilobytes per second.

Licensing agreement
Permission given by a copyright holder that conveys the right to use the copyright holder's work.

Merger doctrine
A concept applied when there are very limited ways to express an idea, so the expression cannot be copyrighted.

Meta
A Greek word meaning one level up.

Meta search engine
A search engine that searches other search engines.

Meta tags
HTML tags containing keywords of a Web site.

MhZ
Megahertz.

Moral rights
Rights of an author to have attribution and integrity rights.

MOV
QuickTime Movie.

MP3
Moving Pictures Expert Group Layer-3 Audio.

MPEG
Motion Pictures Expert Group.

Non-exclusive
A license that can be purchased by several users.

Open access
A license where the author retains copyright but allows use of the work by others.

Optimization
Selecting a file format that reduces file size while preserving quality.

Original work
A distinctive work.

Packet switching protocol
A transmission format that breaks up messages into discrete packets.

Patent law
Provides a monopoly of protection for inventions that meet the requirement of utility, nonobviousness, and novelty.

Photoblog
A photo-based blog.

Podcasting
Audio files of music, news, and so on that are downloadable at the user's convenience.

PPC
Pay per click; sites that pay a search engine to be listed and then pay the search engine a fee when a user visits their site; *same as* search advertising.

PPI
Pixels per inch.

Protocol
A previously agreed-upon standard that determines how computers communicate their data to each other.

Public domain
Any work that no longer has copyright protection.

Relevancy algorithm
A mathematical formula used to match keywords to an index.

Resolution
The amount of clarity and detail in an image.

Rights-managed
The right to use purchased images in a geographical location and for a specific amount of time.

Right of privacy
The right to be left alone.

Right of publicity
The right to control the commercial use of your identity.

Royalty
Payment made to copyright holders for use of their work.

Royalty-free agreement
A purchased license to use a copyright holder's work multiple times and for an unlimited amount of time.

RSS
Rich Site Summary *or* Really Simple Syndication.

Script
Programming language inserted into HTML that spiders cannot search.

Search advertising
Sites that pay a search engine to be listed and then pay the search engine a fee when a user visits them; *same as* PPC.

Search criteria
The words and operators in a search statement.

SEO
Search engine optimization.

Spider
A specific bot that follows each hyperlink to find incidence of keywords; *same as* crawler.

Streaming audio *or* **Streaming video**
Audio or video on the Internet that can be received and played without downloading.

Substantial similarity
The degree to which a second work resembles the original copyrighted work.

Tags
Keywords you can assign to photos to cross-reference them.

Tangible medium of expression
The material object in which a work can be experienced.

TCP/IP
Transmission Control Protocol/Internet Protocol.

Terms of use
The rules copyright owners set for use of their work.

Trade dress law
Protects the appearance and size of a product or service.

Trade secret law
State-governed laws protecting secret formulas, recipes, or processes.

Trademark law
Protects an image, word, symbol, or design used to identify goods and services.

Transformative work
Work transformed by intangible input to be considered as fair use.

UCC
Universal Copyright Convention.

URL
Uniform Resource Locator.

USENET
Early chat room network.

Vector
A line that can be rescaled mathematically—resolution independent.

Vicarious infringement
When a person or entity has direct control of the infringing activity and benefits financially from the infringement.

WAV
Windows Wave.

WIPO
World Intellectual Property Organization.

Work of authorship
The categories of work that are afforded copyright protection.

WWW
World Wide Web.

XML
Extensible markup language.

A1 Free Sound Effects Web site, 150
A & M Records, Inc, v. Napster, Inc., 44
Acuff-Rose v. Campbell, 60,
    Jostens suit, 70
Adobe Photoshop, 61
Adobe Portable Document Format (PDF), 106
advanced searches, 99–104
advertising, conflict with search engines, 88
aggregators, using for RSS feeds, 141
agreements, licensing. See license agreements
AIF (Audio Interchange Format) files, 132
'All Rights Reserved,' 138
AltaVista search engine, 84
American Memory collection, Library of
    Congress, 155–156
AND Boolean operator, 100–101
animated GIFs, 129
animations, finding on the Web, 136–137
AOL Time Warner, song ownership, 47–48
Aqua andMattel case, 61–62
Archie search engine, 85, 86
ARPA (Advanced Research Projects Agency)
    and the Internet, 78
Arriba Soft Corporation case, 47
art
    clip, searching the Web for, 134–135
    photographing in museums, 140
Artist Formerly Known as Prince, 45–46
assets, intangible, 5
Astaire, Fred, 52
attribution, and copyright, 28
audio
    See also music, sound
    common file formats, extensions,
        131–132
    finding files, 149–152
Audio Interchange Format (AIF) files, 132
authenticity, and watermarks, 34

author
    copyright protection issues, 23–25
    defined, 12
avatars, celebrity, 50
AVI (Audio Video Interleaved) file format, 131

Ball, Harvey, 22
bandwidth
    described, 80
    hotlinking, 137
Barbie infringement cases, 61–62, 65–66
Barraud, Francis, 58–59
Barry, John, 12
Basic Books, 60–61
Beastie Boys case, 45
Bell, Alexander, 81
Berne Convention and copyright law, 29–31
Berners-Lee, Tim, 81
bitmap images, 129, 130
blogs, posting photos, images on, 139–140
Blues Foundation, 20
Bluetooth wireless, 82
Boolean operators, using in searches,
    100–101
bootlegging live performances, 149
Bosely Bobbers, 51
bots described, 87
bowdlerization and copyright law, 19
British copyright law, 11–12
browsers and media file formats, 131–132
Burton, Brian and Capital Records case,
    124, 125

Capital Records and Brian Burton case,
    124, 125

cartoon characters and copyright protection,
    28, 48–49
case law
    See also specific cases
    copyright law, 16–17
    digital copying, file sharing decision
        (table), 44
    fair use cases, 59–60
    infringement cases, 65–66
cease-and-desist letters, 66, 124
celebrities and right of publicity and privacy,
    49–52
Cerf, Vinton, 80
Chiffons and George Harrison case, 45
Chilling Effects Clearinghouse, 66–67, 124
China, first copyright protection, 7
Classroom Guidelines (CONTU) for copying,
    57–58
clip art, searching the Web for, 134–13
Clipart Connection home page, 135
clustering search engine results, 93
Communications Decency Act, 82
compilations and copyright protection, 24
compression, MP3 audio, 132
computer network protocols, 79, 80
computers
    See also digital technology
    Internet. *See* Internet
Comstock image site, 120
CONFU (Conference on Fair Use), safe harbor
    guidelines, 57–58
CONTU guidelines, 57
Constitution, U.S. and origin of intellectual
    property law, 6
contract law, license agreements, 27
Contributory infringement, 43
Copyright Act of 1870, 153
Copyright Act of 1909, 22

Copyright Act of 1976, 16, 27, 42
copyright-free, 119–120
    copyright law
    acquiring different licenses, 125–127
    balancing protection and innovation, 21
    copyright protection issues, 19–20,
        22–26
    copyright registration, 32–33
    copyright symbols (table), 9
    copyright transfer, 26
    evolution of, 11–12
    history of, 4
    and hotlinking bandwidth, 137
    infringement. *See* infringement
    international copyright, 29–31
    Internet innovations and, 45–46
    posting copyright notices, 34
    ramifications of law and court cases,
        16–18
    relinquishment of protection, 70
    significant changes in U.S. (table), 13–15
    work for hire, 26–27
Copyright Statute, 28
copyrights
    abandoning, 70
    what to do if you infringe, 66–67
costs of registering copyrights, 33
court cases. *See* case law
crawlers described, 87
Creative Commons, 125–126, 152
    licenses (table), 127
criminal liability in infringement cases, 67
CTEA (Sonny Bono Copyright Term Extension
    Act), ramifications, 16–17
cyberrights, 124
cybersquatting, 59

damages in infringement cases, 67
databases, dynamic, and invisible Web,
    105–108
de minims defined, 45
Department of Defense and computer net-
    works, 80
derivative works
    described, 27
    infringement, 46–47
design patents, 9
digital copying, court decisions (table), 44
Digital Electronics Corporation (DEC), 84
Digital Millennium Copyright Act (DMCA), 18
digital technology
    advancing digital preservation, 147
    digital medium and tangible medium of
        expression, 25
    ramifications on copyright law, 18
digitized photos, images, 138–139
directory search engines, 87
Dirt Devil company, 52
Discovery Channel clip art, 136–137
Disney. *See* Walt Disney Company
Dixon, Willie, 20
DJ Danger Mouse, 124
DMCA (Digital Millennium Copyright Act), 18
DMOZ Open Directory Project, 92
DNS (Domain Name System) and Web
    addresses, 82
Dogpile meta search engine, 93, 142
donation, abandoning copyright by, 70
dynamic databases, and invisible Web,
    105–108

education and fair use, 53–54, 56–58, 60
Eldred, Eric, 17
Eldred v. Ashcroft infringement case, 16–17

Electronic Frontier Foundation, 124
Ellworth, Annie, 81
Else, Jon, 123
Elvis Presley Enterprises, 50–51
EMI music, 125
Encapsulated PostScript (.eps) files, 130
End License User Agreement (EULA),
    Microsoft Office, 134
Ericsson electronics, 82
exclusive license agreements, 120
Extensible Markup Language (XML) and RSS
    feeds, 140–141
extensions, file, 129, 130

factual works, fair use and, 54
fair dealing, 53
fair use doctrine, 7, 42, 53–56
Family Entertainment and Copyright Act of
    2005 (FECA), 18, 19
fan fiction and copyright protection, 28, 55
FECA (Family Entertainment and Copyright Act
    of 2005), 18, 19
federal government Web sites, using
    resources of, 141–142
*Feist Publications v. Rural Telephone Service
    Company,* 24
fiction, fan, and copyright, 28
file extensions
    common graphic (table), 130
    common multimedia (table), 131
file servers and ftp in URL, 85
file-sharing infringement cases, 65
file-sharing software
    copyright protection issues, 21
    court decisions (table), 44
File Transfer Protocol (FTP), 84, 85

files
> *See also* media files
> determining if you can use, 116–118
> finding audio, 149–152
> finding movie, 147–148
> types, extensions, 129–132
filing patents, 8
filters, image content, 142
finding
> *See also* searching
> audio, movie files, 149–152
> music files, 151–152
> photos with mixed licensing, 144–145
> public domain photos, 142–143
FindLaw Web site, 124
Flickr photo-sharing service, 144–145
Ford, Gerald, 55
Ford Motor Company, 50
formats, file, 129–132
Forsythe, Tom, 62, 65
Fox Broadcasting company, 123
freelancers and works for hire, 26–27
Frito Lay and right of publicity violations, 50
FTP (File Transfer Protocol), 84, 85

GATT (General Agreement of Tariffs and
> Trade), 30
Gallery of the Open Frontier, 138, 139
*Getting Permission: How to License and
> Clear Copyrighted Material Online and
> Off* (Stim), 124
GIF file format, 129, 130
Girl Scouts 47–48
GNU, and open source, 118
Google search engine, 86–87, 92, 97, 99
government Web sites
> searching for public domain photos, 146
> using resources of, 141–142

Gracie Films, 123
graphical user interface (GUI), 81, 83
Graphics Interchange Format (GIF), 129, 130
Grey Album (Jay-z), 124
guilt, proving in infringement cases, 64–66
Guthrie, Woody, 49

Hanna-Barbera, 48–49
'Happy Birthday' song, 47–48
Harrison, George, 45
Harry Potter, 55
Hill, Mildred and Patty, 47–48
history of
> copyright law, 4, 11–12
> the Internet, 76–84
holograms as authenticity marks, 34
Hormel Foods, 84
hotlinking bandwidth, 137
HTML (Hypertext Markup Language), 81
HTML pages, bypassing with spiders, 106
HTTP (Hypertext Transfer Protocol)
> described, 82
> and FTP, 85
Hubble Telescope photos, 146
hyperlinking
> and copyright violation, 47
> and the Web, 83
hypertext, history of, 80–81
Hypertext Markup Language (HTML), 81
Hypertext Transfer Protocol. *See* HTTP

ideas, copyright protection of, 22–23
Idea-Expression Dichotomy, 7
images
> finding and acquiring, generally, 116–118
> finding Library of Congress, National
>> Archives, 153–154

and license agreements, 119–120
optimization and resolution, 133
photographs. *See* photographs
restricting content in searches, 142
searching, 102
terms of use, 121–122
index search engines, 86–87
infringement
> copyright, 43–46, 122
> and derivative works, 46–47
> described, 42, 43
> fan fiction and, 27, 55
> Internet innovations and, 47–49
> legalities of, proving suits, 64–67
> music cases. *See* music
> remedies, 67
> right of publicity and privacy, 9, 49–50
> rights (table), 44
> what to do if sued, 66–67, 124–126
injunctions in infringement cases, 67
innovation vs. protection in copyright law, 21
intangible assets and intellectual property, 5
integrity and copyright protection, 28
intellectual property
> categories of, 7–9
> described, 5
> infringement. *See* infringement
> origins of law, 6
> regulatory bodies governing (fig.), 10
international copyright
> described, 29–31
> public domain, 70
Internet
> development and history of the, 76–84
> innovations and copyright law, 47–49
> searching the, 76–77
> vs. the Web, 83–84
Internet Archive, The, 147
Internet Service Providers. *See* ISPs

inventions and intellectual property, 5
invisible Web, searching, 105–108
IRC (Internet Relay Chat), 85
ISPs (Internet Service Providers)
    described, 81
    infringement exception to, 44

Joint Photographic Experts Group (JPEG) file
    format, 129, 130
Jostens (class ring company), 70
JPEG file format, 129, 130

Kahn, Bob, 80
Kelly, Leslie, 47
keywords
    performing searches using, 95–98
    in search text, 87
    using trademarks to trigger
        advertising, 88
Kinko's, 60–61
Koons, Jeff, 63

Lanham Act, 50
law
    See also specific law
    copyright. See copyright law
    intellectual property. See intellectual property
    public domain, 68–70
    trademark. See trademark law
lawsuits, infringement, 64–67, 124–126
Led Zeppelin royalties disputes, 20
leeching, 137
letter, request for permission (fig.), 123
Librarian's Internet Index (LII), 107–108
liability described, 42

libraries
    accessing usable media through, 117
    Library of Congress, 153–158
    Library of Congress, finding media at,
        153–158
license agreements
    acquiring different licenses, 125–127
    Creative Commons' forms for, 126–127
    described, 119–120
    obtaining permission, 122–125
    signing away copyright, 27
    terms of use, 121–122
licensing your work as open access, 125
links
    copyright, 122
    hyperlinks. See hyperlinking
    sponsored, 88
logos and copyright, 63
Loufrani, Franklin, 23

market effect and fair use, 56
Mattel, 61–62, 65, 66
media
    file types, 129–132
    file optimization and resolution, 133
    finding and acquiring, generally, 116
medium of expression, tangible and
    nontangible, 25, 42
merger doctrine, and the public domain,
    68–69
meta search engines, 93
meta tags described, 91
MGM v. Grokster, 44
Mickey Mouse, 49
Microsoft clip art, using, 134
Midler, Bette, 50
Mitchell, Margaret, 60

Morguefile.com, 128
Morse, Samuel, 81
Motion Pictures Expert Group (MPEG) file
    format, 131
MOV (QuickTime Movie) file format, 131
Movie Entertainment OnLine, 147
movie file formats, 131
movies
    See also video
    and fair use, 58
    finding movie files, 147–148
MP3 (Moving Pictures Expert Group Layer-3
    Audio) file format, 132
MPEG (Motion Pictures Expert Group) file
    format, 131
museums, photographing art in, 140
music
    Acuff-Rose Music and Roy Orbison case, 70
    bootlegging live performances, 149
    case law. See specific cases, appellants
    and copyright protection, 24–25
    downloaded music suit, 65
    finding on the Web, 151–152
    George Harrison and The Chiffons
        case, 45
    Led Zeppelin royalties disputes, 20
    online, and copyright law, 18
    royalties disputes, 20
    sampling, and copyright, 27
    2 Live Crew and Roy Orbison case, 60

Nation magazine, 55
National Archives, finding media at, 154
New York Public Library, 138–139
news reporting and fair use, 53–54
Newton v. Diamond, 45
Nixon, Richard, 55

Nolo Press, books on public domain and
obtaining permission, 124
non-exclusive licenses, 120
nonprofit use, 122
NoodleQuest search strategizer, 96
NOT Boolean operator, 100–101

ODP (Open Directory Project), 88
online books and public domain issue, 17
online music
See also music
and intellectual property, 18
open access licenses, 125
open content, open source, 118
Open Directory Project (ODP), 88
operators, using Boolean in searches,
100–101
optimization
image or audio file, 133
search engine optimization (SEO), 90
OR Boolean operator, 100–101
Orbison, Roy, 59, 60
Overture search engine, 92
ownership
copyright, 26–28
and intellectual property, 5

paparazzi and rights of publicity and
privacy, 51
parody and fair use, 53–54, 60
patent filing, politics of, 8–9
patent law described, 7–8
pay-per-click (PPC) searches, 87–88, 92
PD Photo.org, 143–144
PDF files, 106
peer-to-peer (P2P), copyright protection
issues, 21

permission
See also license agreements
obtaining to use content, 122–125
request letter (fig.), 123
personal data, search engines that gather, 88
personal responsibilities and fair use, 56
Philadelphia Spelling Book (Barry), 12
photoblogs, 140
photographs
attaching tags to, 145
finding at the Library of Congress,
155–156
finding on the Web, 138–139
finding public domain, with licensing,
142–145
searching government sites for public
domain, 146
sites for, 120
photomuse.org, 138–139
Photoshop (Adobe), 61
Pickett, Ferdinand, 45
pixels and Web image resolution, 133
plagiarism, student, 56–57
podcasting, 141
Polly, Jean Armour, 84
Portable Networks Graphics (.png) files, 130
posting copyright notices, 34
Potter, Harry, 55
Progress Clause, 17
Presley, Elvis, 50–51
previewing image files, 136
Prince, Artist Formerly Known as, 45–46
printing
images, low and high-resolution, 133
search results, 97
privacy, right of, 9, 49–50
property, intellectual. *See* intellectual property

protection vs. innovation in copyright law, 21
protocols, computer, 79, 80
public domain
and copyright law, 16, 42
dates, when U.S. works pass into (figs.), 17
examples of works in, 68
images in, 138–139
international agreements, 68–70
open content, open source, 118
photos, finding, 142–143, 146
publicity, right of, 9, 50–52

QuickTime Movie file format, 131

Radio Corporation of America (RCA), 59
raster images, 129
Really Simple Syndication (RSS) feeds,
140–141
Recording Industry Association of America
(RIAA), 65
registering
copyrights, 32–33
domain names, and cybersquatting, 59
regulatory bodies governing intellectual
property law (fig.), 10
research and fair use, 53–54
resolution of image or audio files, 133
Rich Site Summary (RSS) feeds, 140–141
right of privacy, 9, 49–50
right of publicity, 9, 50–52
rights
copyright bundle of, 27
infringement (table), 44
of patent holders, 8
signing away copyright, 27